Bess of Hardwick:

Countess of Shrewsbury

A Tudor Times Insight

Copyright © 2019 Tudor Times Ltd

The right of Tudor Times Ltd to be identified as the author of the work has been asserted in accordance with the Copyright, Designs and Patents Act 1988.

This ebook is copyright material and must not be copied, reproduced, transferred, distributed, leased, licensed or publicly performed or used in any way except as specifically permitted in writing by the publishers, as allowed under the terms and conditions under which it was purchased or as strictly permitted by applicable copyright law. Any unauthorised distribution or use of this text may be a direct infringement of the author's and publisher's rights, and those responsible may be liable in law accordingly.

First published by Tudor Times Ltd in 2019

www.tudortimes.co.uk

Tudor Times Insights

Tudor Times Insights collate articles from our website www.tudortimes.co.uk which is a repository for a wide variety of information about the Tudor and Stewart period 1485 – 1625. There you can find material on People, Places, Daily Life, Military & Warfare, Politics & Economics and Religion. The site has a Book Review section, with author interviews and a book club. It also features comprehensive family trees, and a 'What's On' event list with information about forthcoming activities relevant to the Tudors and Stewarts.

Titles in the Series

Profiles

Katherine Parr: Henry VIII's Sixth Queen

James IV: King of Scots

Lady Margaret Pole: Countess of Salisbury

Thomas Wolsey: Henry VIII's Cardinal

Thomas Cromwell: Henry VIII's Chief Minister

Marie of Guise: Regent of Scotland

James V: Scotland's Renaissance King

Lady Penelope Devereux: Sir Philip Sidney's Muse

Lady Katherine Grey: Tudor Prisoner

Sir William Cecil: Elizabeth I's Chief Minister

Lady Margaret Douglas: Countess of Lennox

Sir James Melville: Scottish Ambassador

Tudors & Stewarts 2015

Lady Margaret Beaufort: Tudor Matriarch
James, Earl of Moray: Regent of Scotland
Mary I: Queen of England
Jasper Tudor: Brother & Uncle of Kings
Katharine of Aragon: Henry VIII's First Wife
Honor Grenville: Lady Lisle
James VI & I: First King of Great Britain
Margaret Tudor: Queen of Scots

Politics & Economy
The Field of Cloth of Gold
Succession: The Tudor Problem
The Pilgrimage of Grace & Exeter Conspiracy

Contents

Preface 7

Family Tree 8

Part 1: Bess of Hardwick's Life Story 9

    Chapter 1: Youth and First Marriage 9

    Chapter 2: Lady Cavendish 12

    Chapter 3: Debts 16

    Chapter 4: Widow and Countess 19

    Chapter 5: Countess and Warder 22

    Chapter 6: Guarding the Queen of Scots 26

    Chapter 7: Family Arrangements 29

    Chapter 8: Royal Wrath 32

    Chapter 9: Financial Worries 35

    Chapter 10: More Financial Affairs 38

    Chapter 11: Marital Disputes 42

    Chapter 12: Vicious Rumour 46

    Chapter 13: Royal Commission 48

    Chapter 14: A Trip to London 52

    Chapter 15: Hardwick 55

    Chapter 16: Last Years 59

Part 2: Aspects of Bess of Hardwick's Life 63

    Chapter 17: Following the Footsteps of Bess of Hardwick 63

Chapter 18: Bess the Networker 76

Chapter 19: Dowries and Marriage Settlements 87

Chapter 19: Book Review 96

Bibliography 99

Preface

Bess of Hardwick rose from obscurity to be one of the richest women in England and a friend of Elizabeth I. Her story is one of determination, grit, ambition and clever management. Born a poor gentleman farmer's daughter, she died a countess and grandmother to a possible heir to the throne. Bess married four times, and was sincerely attached to all her husbands, although her final marriage disintegrated under unbearable pressures.

Like most Tudor women, Bess never left England, but she travelled regularly between her native Derbyshire and London, and to the estates of her third husband in Somerset, as well as with the court. Many of her journeys related to supervision of her magnificent constructions at Chatsworth and Hardwick.

A clever and practical woman, she used the law to protect herself and her family and to build a huge inheritance for the dynasty she founded. She amassed a vast fortune and her descendants have held high positions in English society for 400 years.

Family Tree

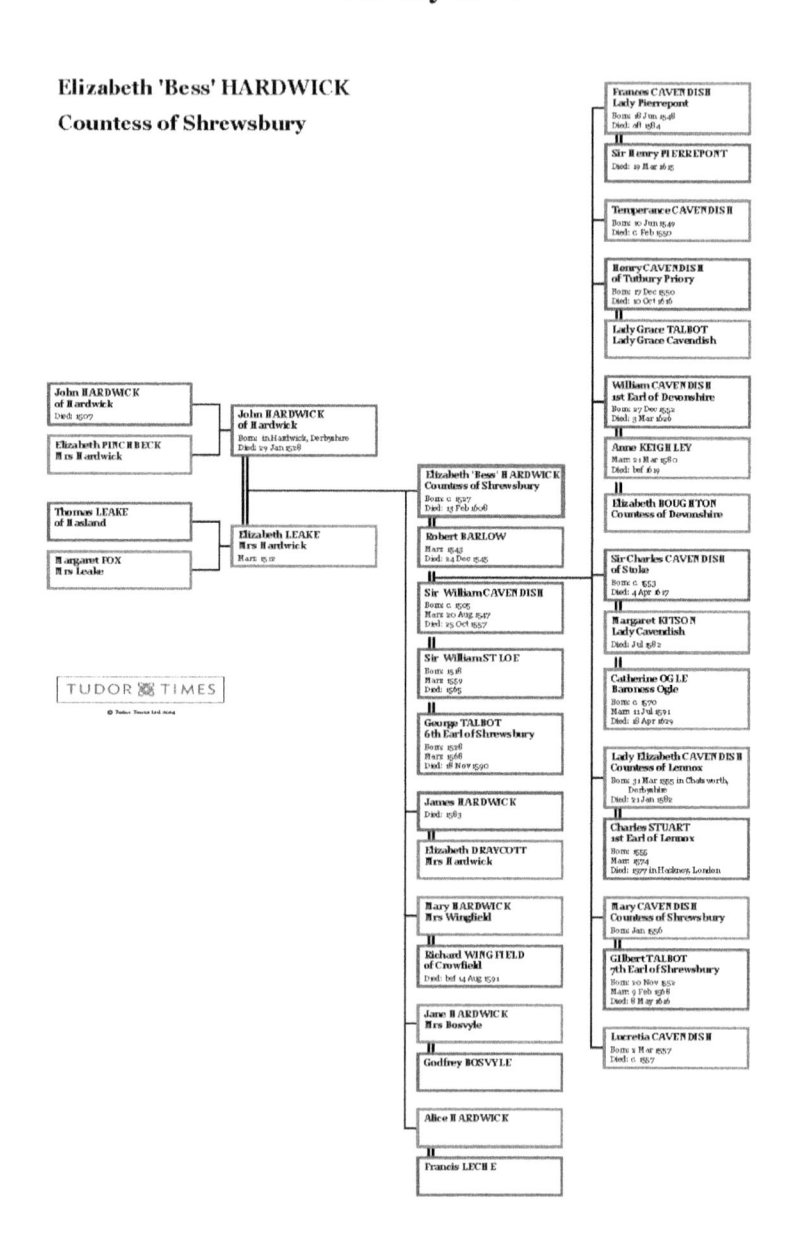

Elizabeth 'Bess' HARDWICK, Countess of Shrewsbury

John HARDWICK of Hardwick
Died: 1507

Elizabeth PINCHBECK Mrs Hardwick

Thomas LEAKE of Hasland

Margaret FOX Mrs Leake

John HARDWICK of Hardwick
Born: in Hardwick, Derbyshire
Died: 29 Jan 1528

Elizabeth LEAKE Mrs Hardwick
Marr: 1520

Children of John Hardwick and Elizabeth Leake:

Elizabeth 'Bess' HARDWICK, Countess of Shrewsbury
Born: c. 1527
Died: 13 Feb 1608

- **Robert BARLOW** — Marr: 1543; Died: 24 Dec 1545
- **Sir William CAVENDISH** — Born: c. 1505; Marr: 20 Aug 1547; Died: 25 Oct 1557
- **Sir William ST LOE** — Born: 1518; Marr: 1559; Died: 1565
- **George TALBOT, 6th Earl of Shrewsbury** — Born: 1528; Marr: 1568; Died: 18 Nov 1590

James HARDWICK
Died: 1583

Elizabeth DRAYCOTT Mrs Hardwick

Mary HARDWICK Mrs Wingfield

Richard WINGFIELD of Crowfield
Died: bef 14 Aug 1591

Jane HARDWICK Mrs Bosvyle

Godfrey BOSVYLE

Alice HARDWICK

Francis LECHE

Children of Bess Hardwick and Sir William Cavendish:

Frances CAVENDISH, Lady Pierrepont
Born: 16 Jun 1548
Died: 08 1613

- **Sir Henry PIERREPONT** — Died: 29 Mar 1615

Temperance CAVENDISH
Born: 10 Jun 1549
Died: c. Feb 1550

Henry CAVENDISH of Tutbury Priory
Born: 17 Dec 1550
Died: 10 Oct 1616

- **Lady Grace TALBOT, Lady Grace Cavendish**

William CAVENDISH, 1st Earl of Devonshire
Born: 27 Dec 1552
Died: 3 Mar 1626

- **Anne KEIGHLEY** — Marr: 21 Mar 1582; Died: bef 1619
- **Elizabeth BOUGHTON, Countess of Devonshire**

Sir Charles CAVENDISH of Stoke
Born: 1553
Died: 4 Apr 1617

- **Margaret KITSON, Lady Cavendish** — Died: Jul 1582
- **Catherine OGLE, Baroness Ogle** — Born: c. 1570; Marr: 12 Jul 1591; Died: 18 Apr 1629

Lady Elizabeth CAVENDISH, Countess of Lennox
Born: 31 Mar 1555 in Chatsworth, Derbyshire
Died: 21 Jan 1582

- **Charles STUART, 1st Earl of Lennox** — Born: 1555; Marr: 1574; Died: 1577 in Hackney, London

Mary CAVENDISH, Countess of Shrewsbury
Born: Jan 1556

- **Gilbert TALBOT, 7th Earl of Shrewsbury** — Born: 20 Nov 1552; Marr: 9 Feb 1568; Died: 8 May 1616

Lucretia CAVENDISH
Born: 2 Mar 1557
Died: c. 1557

© Tudor Times Ltd. 2014

Part 1: Bess of Hardwick's Life Story

Chapter 1: Youth and First Marriage

Elizabeth, or Bess, as she is popularly known, was born during the early 1520s to John Hardwick, a small landowner of Hardwick, Derbyshire, and Elizabeth Leake. Her actual birthdate is unknown – from as early as 1521 to as late as 1527 have been postulated.

The Hardwicks had been established at Hardwick Hall for generations – their relatives were solid members of the gentry class, who married between themselves and passed on their well-cultivated acres to the eldest son, with a comfortable dowry in cash or goods for daughters. But when Bess' father died in early 1528, the family was thrown into turmoil. The heir, her brother James, was only two years old, and immediately became a ward of the king himself.

During a ward's youth, his lands would be administered by whomever the king granted the wardship to. Although the lands could not be diminished, the income went into the pocket of the guardian, who had to provide for the heir. Like many other landowners, John Hardwick sought to give his lands to trustees, but inadequate arrangements had been made by the time of his death, although his will referred to them. Curiously, as there is no evidence of how the relationship came to pass, John Hardwick named the Earl of Shrewsbury as the overseer of his will.

The initial Inquisition Post Mortem, which was always held after the death of a landowner, accepted the arrangements, but the following year a second inspection was held by the Court of Wards and it was held that John had died in full possession of his lands.

The widow was entitled under common law to a third of the income of the land in dower, and from this she had to maintain the younger children. The other two thirds were in the hands of the Court. Some of the land was subject to the jointure rights of another individual, and the remainder was divided – part was retained by the Crown and probably leased back to Elizabeth Hardwick, and the remainder, together with the wardship of James Hardwick, was sold to an official. Once James reached the age of twenty-one, he could sue out his livery and retake possession.

Within a couple of years of her widowhood, Elizabeth remarried. Her second husband, Ralph Leche, was a younger son of a family of similar standing, although he, too, had little income. From this marriage, a further three daughters were born. The similarity of his name to Elizabeth's maiden name suggests he was a connection – spelling was not consistent and phonemes were spelt in various ways.

Despite their precarious financial situation, the family had good connections, and Bess was placed in the household of Anne Gainsford, Lady Zouche. There is no contemporary evidence for this, but Bess' two main biographers believe the circumstantial evidence is realistic. The Zouches of Codnor were distant relatives, and the custom of placing young people in families of higher social standing was universal. Lady Zouche had been a maid of honour to Queen Anne Boleyn and it was allegedly she who had introduced the queen to William Tyndale's *Obedience of Christian Man* with impressive results. If Lady Zouche was a committed Evangelical, that would certainly explain Bess' own firmly Protestant views, despite her origins in an area of the country that clung to the old faith.

At some time before 28th May 1543, Bess married for the first time. She was probably about fifteen, and her husband was younger. Although early marriages were not uncommon, it is surprising in this case, where Bess' dowry under her father's will was not extensive (around 40 – 60 marks, depending on how the will interpreted) and her new husband, Robert Barlow, was a minor, and also a Ward of Court. It has been suggested that the early marriage was arranged by Robert's dying father to keep the one-third of the estate that Bess would have had as jointure, out of the Court of Wards, and prevent any guardian to whom Robert's wardship was sold getting control of the whole estate.

The whole thing is clouded in the usual complex monetary negotiations of the time, with debts and contra-debts being cancelled and sums paid backward and forward. When Barlow senior died, Robert's wardship was bought by George Bosvyle, who was betrothed to Bess' sister, Jane Hardwick.

As a married woman, Bess had more status than previously, but nothing is known of the couple's life together, or even where they lived. It is unlikely, in view of the groom's age, that the marriage was consummated. In any event, there were no children before Robert died on 24th December 1544.

Chapter 2: Lady Cavendish

Bosvyle lost his investment, as Robert's heir was his younger brother, George. Bess was entitled to her dower, but the new guardian of the estates declined to pay. Even at the age of sixteen, Bess would not be deprived of her rights and took the matter to court. The matter became mired in legal claim and counter-claim with an interim settlement forced upon her in 1545. Eventually, in 1553, she won her claim and became entitled to a very comfortable dower – significantly greater than her father's estate had been.

During this period her living arrangements are unknown – possibly the Barlow home, as, despite her case against the guardian, Sir Peter Frecheville, she was on good terms with the family, possibly her mother's home (although Ralph Leche was in prison for debt) or even back to Lady Zouche initially.

It is likely that before 1547, Bess joined the household of the Marchioness of Dorset, at Bradgate Park in Leicestershire. Lady Dorset had been born Lady Frances Brandon, and was Henry VIII's niece and her husband, Henry Grey, Marquess of Dorset, was a very distant connection of the Hardwicks.

This introduced Bess to royal circles, and also maintained her Protestant outlook. The Marquess was a leading light amongst reformers, and his daughter, Lady Jane Grey, took after him.

Whilst Bess was in the Dorset household, she married the widowed Sir William Cavendish of Chatsworth. Sir William, who had daughters by a previous marriage, had been in court circles all his life. His brother, George Cavendish, is famous for his *Life of Thomas Wolsey*. William worked with Cromwell on the Dissolution of the Monasteries and was a clerk in the Office of Augmentations (responsible for the realisation of the value of monastic land for the Crown).

Like many others who worked in Augmentations, Cavendish spotted some excellent bargains and made the best of his position. He held a number of posts and was eventually appointed as a Privy Councillor in 1546. Sir William was twenty years older than Bess, so, although she may well have liked him, the match would have been primarily for an increase in status and security. She would not be the first young woman to marry an older, wealthier man, nor he the first man to look for a young step-mother for his children.

Bess was now mistress of her own household. She had a country estate at Northaw, and a London house near St Paul's. Children arrived at yearly intervals starting with Frances, on 18th June 1548. The child was named after her godmother, Lady Dorset, and her other godmother was Katherine Willoughby, Dowager Duchess of Suffolk, whilst Lady Dorset's half-brother, the Duke of Suffolk was godfather.

Bess' biographer, David Durant, sees these godparents as merely friends without political influence, but the reality was that Lady Dorset's children had been named as heirs to the throne by Henry VIII after his own children. Whilst Dorset was not a member of the Council guiding the realm during the minority of King Edward, he was still one of the premier noblemen in the land.

Bess' second child, Temperance, born within the year, also had illustrious god-parents – Jane, Lady Warwick (soon to be Duchess of Northumberland), Lady Jane Grey and Francis Talbot, 5th Earl of Shrewsbury. Such grand sponsors did not ensure the baby's health, and she died within a few months.

Cavendish and Bess had plenty of ready cash, and in the summer of 1549, they bought a large parcel of land near Bess' childhood home in Derbyshire, centred on the village of Chatsworth. They then increased their holdings in the area by exchanges of properties that Cavendish held in other counties. This concentration of their wealth in one location continued. To avoid the problems of wardship that Bess had experienced at first hand, their lands were held in survivorship, reducing the likelihood that their heir would inherit as a minor.

This son and heir, Henry, arrived in 1550 and his godparents were even more illustrious than his older sisters' – including the Lady Elizabeth, half-sister to the King, as well as Dorset (soon Duke of Suffolk) and Warwick (shortly thereafter Duke of Northumberland). A further four children followed, and the roll call of their godparents shows that the Cavendishes were friends with some of the most influential people in England and the accounts, both monetary and descriptive, suggest a busy social whirl, with parties, holiday fun, heavy gambling and the observation of traditional customs such as May Day and the Lord of Misrule.

In 1551, the Cavendishes began their first major building project with the initiation of construction of a new manor house at Chatsworth.

But in 1553, what had looked like good policy in selecting friends, was suddenly very risky, when Edward VI attempted to change the succession as laid down in the Act of Succession of 1543 to pass over his sisters and put Lady Jane Grey, Suffolk's daughter, on the throne. The legal heir, the Lady Mary, was having none of it, and achieved a swift triumph. Bess' old friend, Frances, begged for her life and Suffolk's, and Mary spared them, but Northumberland was executed and the Cavendishes were suspected of complicity, although no action was taken against them.

In a bid to restore themselves to royal favour, Queen Mary was invited to stand as godmother to Bess' second son, Charles – alongside Suffolk! The next child had Suffolk's second daughter, Lady Katherine Grey, as godmother. Durant sees this as a brave loyalty to their friends, and describes Lady Katherine as an outcast following the execution of Suffolk and Lady Jane after Wyatt's rebellion, but, in fact, Lady Katherine was a maid-of-honour to the queen.

For the majority of Mary's reign, Bess remained at Chatsworth, supervising the extravagant building works, although William had also leased a house at Brentford from Sir John Thynne of Longleat, and it was there that her daughter, Elizabeth, was born.

Chapter 3: Debts

Having avoided trouble in 1553, in 1557, Sir William was accused of embezzlement of Crown funds. It was expected that royal officials would cream off a certain level of profit from their positions but the Treasurer, Sir William Paulet, obviously felt that Cavendish had gone too far – and the scale of their land purchases and living expenses suggest that too much money was sticking to Cavendish's fingers. It was not the first time Cavendish had been accused of false accounting: back in his days of visiting and dissolving monasteries, questions had been raised about a claim for some non-existent expenses.

Bess, who had been in Derbyshire for some time, returned to London whilst William tried to work on his defence. Before he could either be punished or pardoned, William died, leaving Bess a widow for the second time on 25th October 1557.

Unfortunately, Sir William's debts did not die with him, and the following spring a bill was brought into Parliament, the substance of which was for the confiscation of the estate to pay the amount of £5,000 that her late husband was accused of misappropriating. The bill was not specific to Bess, but had wider application.

In despair, she wrote to Sir John Thynne, an old friend, from whom she and William had leased a house in Brentford. Whether through the eloquence of Thynne or because the bill would damage too many others, it was not passed. Whilst Bess was still in debt to the Crown, she could try to find another way to deal with the situation.

As 1558 progressed, it became clear that Queen Mary would have no child of her own, and that the next monarch would be the Lady Elizabeth. Whilst Elizabeth was not attached to her Grey cousins, she was part of the wider circle around them, including the Dudleys and Sir William Cecil, who were all friends of Bess. Elizabeth, it may be remembered, had also been godmother to one of Bess' children. It is likely that during 1558, Bess was spending as much time as possible keeping her relationship with Elizabeth warm, and probably visiting her at Hatfield from time to time.

Mary died on 17th November, and Elizabeth was proclaimed queen. It is likely that Bess was either at Hatfield or nearby at the time. Soon after, Bess was appointed as a lady-in-waiting. One of the new queen's other appointees was an acquaintance of Bess, Sir William St Loe (also spelt St Loo, Saintlowe, Sentlowe etc.) He was appointed as the Captain of the Queen's Guard and Chief Butler.

St Loe, who was around seven years older than Bess, had had a solid career, first as part of the endless English military manoeuvres in Ireland, and then with a place in the household, first of Henry VIII and then Edward VI. On that King's death, he became one of Elizabeth's gentlemen. St Loe was a committed

Protestant and in 1554 he was sent to the Tower on suspicion of involvement in Wyatt's Rebellion. Although suspected of passing messages between Wyatt's men and Elizabeth, he never admitted to anything, and was eventually fined and released.

He was now given his reward. As well as the offices granted by Elizabeth, St Loe held good lands in Somerset. These lands were to be matter of an ongoing dispute between him and his next brother, Edward St Loe.

In July 1559, St Loe and Bess announced their betrothal. They were married on 27th August, either in London, or at the groom's home of Sutton Court, Chew Magna, Somerset. They were certainly at Sutton Court a few weeks later as the new Lady St Loe gave orders for building works, before the couple returned to the capital.

Building was becoming a passion with Bess. As well as ordering works at Sutton Court, she was continuing the major build at Chatsworth, which was now ready for the decorative plastering that was the fashion of the age.

Before long, the comfortable married life that Bess was settling into with a husband whose letters suggest that he was deeply in love with her, ran into problems. Edward St Loe claimed that his father had told Edward's second wife, Margaret Scutt, that Sutton Court should form part of her jointure, but he could produce no documentary evidence. William St Loe suggested a compromise. He would not give up ownership, but Edward and his wife could live at Sutton Court, with Edward acting as Steward. Edward departed, not entirely satisfied, and almost before the dust had settled, Bess fell ill. It was believed she had been poisoned.

William's thoughts leapt to his brother, and even their mother thought Edward the guilty party. Investigations brought to light a '*necromancer*', Hugh Draper, who was thought to be Edward's accomplice. At this point, Bess' biographers differ. Lovell believes that a cousin of William's, another Elizabeth St Loe, was confined to the Tower as part of this conspiracy to poison William and Bess, whilst Durant identifies this prisoner quite differently.

There was further argument between the brothers, which resulted in a complex court case, following which, Edward's wife, Margaret St Loe, nee Scutt, was granted Sutton Court for her life time. Following this, William rearranged his financial affairs to make Bess his main beneficiary. Previously, Bess had been very happy for Edward to be his brother's heir, but, with the suspicion that he might anticipate nature, and the very ugly wrangling over Sutton Court, it was important for any incentive to be removed.

Chapter 4: Widow and Countess

In August 1561, it is possible that Bess became involved in another scandal. Lady Katherine Grey, second daughter of Bess' old mistress, Lady Frances, had secretly married the Earl of Hertford. For a member of the royal family (and many believed

Lady Katherine to be Elizabeth's heir) to marry without consent was treason. Hertford was abroad, so Katherine, finding herself to be pregnant, needed to find a friend to plead her cause with the queen.

Both Dunant and Lovell record that Lady Katherine confided her secret to Bess, who, horrified, refused to have anything to do with it. Dunant believes that Bess was questioned and committed to the Tower, spending 31 weeks there, being released on 25th March 1562. According to Lovell, Bess was questioned, but not held, and remained on such good terms with the queen that she received a New Year's gift. This interpretation tends to be supported by two letters written to Bess, one in November 1561, thanking her for hospitality, addressed to her in London, the other the following May, addressed to her at Chatsworth, although the November letter could refer to an event prior to any imprisonment.

Lady Katherine's biographer, Leanda de Lisle, identifies the Elizabeth St Loe in whom Lady Katherine confided as the cousin, whom Lovell has in the Tower. Our interpretation would be that it is far more likely that Lady Katherine would confide in her old friend – she was godmother to one of Bess' children. The slight flaw in that argument is that the woman is referred to as 'Mistress' St Loe, not Lady, but these things were not always consistent. Make of it what you will!

In 1563, the problem of the debt that Bess had inherited from William Cavendish was substantially reduced, when it was pardoned by Elizabeth on payment of a fine of £1,000 by St Loe, on behalf of his wife, and her son, Henry Cavendish.

Bess' three sons went to Eton, and her eldest daughter, Frances, went into the household of the Pierreponts, before being married to one of the Pierrepont sons. Bess spent much of her time at Chatsworth, whilst St Loe was often required to be at court – Elizabeth did not like to be neglected for the sake of wives. The evidence from their letters is that Bess and her husband were deeply attached to each other. There is no record of their feelings about the lack of children, when both had had children by previous marriages, but presumably, it was a disappointment. In particular, St Loe, who had only daughters, would probably have liked to have a son to inherit.

The couple spent the Christmas of 1564 at court, and Bess remained there until early February when she was called back to Derbyshire to deal with family problems. Her brother, James, was in debt and ill, and wished to borrow money. Bess therefore returned home. Shortly after arriving, she was obliged to immediately go back to London – St Loe was seriously ill.

William died before Bess could see him again. She must have been horrified to learn that Edward St Loe had been with him, but there was no mention of poison, and St Loe was buried in the Church of Great St Helen's in Bishopsgate.

Within weeks, St Loe's will was being contested by Margaret Norton, his daughter by his first wife. Unsurprisingly, there was sympathy for St Loe's daughters, completely excluded from his will, and Bess' reputation suffered.

The matter of Sutton Court was now reopened in a Somerset court. Edward St Loe claiming that, on his deathbed, William had given Margaret St Loe a life interest in Sutton Court (because Edward and William's father had once promised it to her in jointure). It was alleged by the St Loes that Bess had malignly influenced her husband in order to wrest away the ancient St Loe inheritance. The upshot was that Margaret was granted Sutton Court for life, with remainder to Bess. Rather hard on William's daughters!

With this unhappy event behind her, Bess, now more than comfortably off, returned to Chatsworth. Her two youngest daughters were still at home, and she had plenty to do, overseeing more building works.

Bess returned to court during the summer of 1566 and before long there was speculation about remarriage – Sir John Thynne, who had previously helped her, was one possibility mentioned, along with Lords Darcy and Cobham. But Bess could do better than that. In late 1567, she made her most splendid match of all. Her fourth husband, recently widowed thirty-nine year old George Talbot, was one of the richest men in the country, and an earl. Bess was now Countess of Shrewsbury.

Chapter 5: Countess and Warder

The Earl of Shrewsbury had lands across the Midlands, and, from a practical perspective, these integrated well with Bess' holdings. In addition, he owned Sheffield Castle and Sheffield Manor, Tutbury Castle (leased from the Crown), Worksop Manor, Buxton Hall, and two former abbeys – Rufford and Welbeck. He had a London house and another at Chelsea. Unlike many of the northern nobility, Shrewsbury was firmly Protestant, which, added to his wealth and influence, meant he was one of Elizabeth's most important and trusted councillors in the Midlands and north.

Part of the arrangements included cross-marriages between Bess' children and Shrewsbury's. Her eldest son, Henry, was to marry Lady Grace Talbot, and the expectation was that he would be Bess' main heir. Simultaneously, Mary Cavendish was married to the earl's second son, Gilbert; his oldest, Francis, already having married Lady Anne Herbert, the Earl of Pembroke's daughter. Gilbert and Mary were fourteen and twelve respectively, whilst there was a greater disparity of age between Henry, eighteen, and Grace who was around ten.

To ensure that the marriage arrangements were robust, if any of the siblings died before the marriages had been consummated, they were to be passed on to the next sibling in line. Both marriages were contracted on 19th February 1568 at the Church of St Peter and St Paul in Sheffield. The brides were too young for consummation, but that would follow when they were around fifteen or sixteen.

Although almost all marriages were undertaken for practical and economic reasons, both Bess and Shrewsbury were free to make a choice that was personally pleasing to them, and it is apparent from Shrewsbury's letters to her that he quickly came to love his wife – he regrets her not being with him at nights, during his frequent trips to manage his estates or to serve the queen. In one letter, he refers to a *'faithful affection, which I have not tasted so deeply of before'*, suggesting that he was happier with Bess than he had been with his first wife, Lady Gertrude Manners.

Whilst Shrewsbury and Bess were in the first flush of marital harmony, the queen made arrangements that would eventually destroy their peace. In June 1568, Mary, Queen of Scots escaped Scotland after the loss of the Battle of Langside. She was first held as an *'honoured guest'* at Carlisle, and then at Bolton Castle, whilst Elizabeth considered her options. It soon became apparent that, whatever Elizabeth herself might have preferred, her Councillors were adamant that Mary should neither be allowed to return to Scotland or France, nor brought to the English court.

Instead, the twenty-seven-year-old Mary was to be kept in honourable confinement. It was quickly decided that there was too much sympathy for Mary in the Catholic North, so the decision was taken to put her in the care of the firm Protestant Shrewsbury, in his manor at Tutbury.

As well as Shrewsbury's undoubted loyalty, he had other qualifications – he was immensely wealthy and could support the additional expenses required to entertain and guard a queen, and he was attached to his new wife, so less likely to fall victim to Mary's famous beauty and charm. He was also of sufficient rank to be acceptable to Mary, and, most important of all, his properties were concentrated in the centre of the country, far from any sea coasts.

Mary arrived at Tutbury towards the end of February. Tutbury itself was an old hunting lodge. From the beginning, Mary complained of the damp and cold – within four days, her furniture was sprouting mould. Even worse, the privies were not drained but had to be emptied weekly, the resulting stench infiltrating her windows.

Bess had received a consignment of tapestries, carpets and plate from the royal stores, but had only two weeks' warning to undertake other refurbishment. She had to have bedding and other items sent from her own apartments at Sheffield Castle to make the place habitable.

The Shrewsburys received strict instructions that Mary, whilst she was to be treated as a queen, was not to receive any visitors without permission from the Council (there had been complaints about her holding court at Bolton). She was also supposed to see Bess only occasionally, but within weeks the two were spending considerable amounts of time together, mostly working on embroidery, which was Mary's chief pastime. It was fortunate the queen had both the taste and skill for needlework as her physical activity was extremely curtailed.

Shrewsbury reported to Cecil that Bess and Mary whiled away the hours together, talking on trifling matters. Whilst it had not been intended that Mary should spend much time with Bess, Shrewsbury thought a friendship between them would add to security, rather than endanger it. The results of their hours of work may be seen in the tapestries at Oxburgh Hall.

Mary had her dower as Queen of France, and, as well as using this money to pay the network of secret supporters and spies that she built up over time, she bought furniture for herself and gifts for her '*hosts*'.

Chapter 6: Guarding the Queen of Scots

It soon became apparent that Tutbury was wholly unsuitable for guarding Mary. It was too small to allow sufficient guards to be billeted and the situation of the house was deeply unhealthy. Shrewsbury decided to move her to Wingfield Manor. Bess went ahead to prepare the house in early April 1569. Despite it generally being a healthier house, Mary fell ill. Elizabeth sent doctors – it would not do for Mary to die unexpectedly – and they recommended a move whilst the house was cleaned.

Accordingly, Mary was taken to Bess' own home at Chatsworth for a few nights before returning to Wingfield. At the same time, Shrewsbury himself became extremely ill. So ill, in fact, that Elizabeth sent the Earl of Huntingdon and Sir Ralph Sadler to help Bess keep Mary properly guarded. After an initial recovery, Shrewsbury had a relapse, and Sir John Zouch was sent to help out. Fortunately, the earl recovered.

During the summer of 1569, Mary had been corresponding with the Duke of Norfolk about a possible marriage between them. Norfolk, Elizabeth's cousin, was the senior noble in England, and a Protestant. Many of Elizabeth's Council, including Robert Dudley, Earl of Leicester, her closest friend, thought this an excellent plan and the discussions were widely known. Unfortunately, no-one had told Elizabeth. When she discovered the proposal she reacted furiously. Norfolk was harangued by Elizabeth and sent to the Tower, and Shrewsbury received immediate orders to return Mary to Tutbury, which was more easily guarded.

Within days of Norfolk's arrest, the north of England broke out into revolt under the Earls of Westmorland (Norfolk's brother-in-law) and Northumberland. Hearing that an army was heading south to liberate Mary, the Council quickly sent orders for Shrewsbury to take the Scottish Queen to Coventry. By November, the Mass had been celebrated once more in Durham Cathedral, but by the end of the year, Elizabeth's forces, under the Earl of Sussex, had resulted in the dispersal of the rebels.

Mary was moved back to Tutbury. She now knew that she would never be freed by Elizabeth, and began an endless series of plans and plots to achieve her freedom. Trying to counter her actions, whilst still treating her honourably, and acknowledging that, even if Elizabeth would not openly admit it, Mary was probably the heir to the throne, made Shrewsbury's life a misery, and this began to tell on his relationship with Bess.

After the immediate danger posed by the Rising of the Northern Earls, Mary was finally removed from Tutbury. Over the next fourteen years, she would be carried back and forth between Chatsworth, Sheffield Castle and Wingfield, with Bess and Shrewsbury bearing the brunt of the dislocation of their lives, and the huge expenditure involved. Elizabeth never provided enough cash, and, unsurprisingly, Mary was reluctant to use her dower on the costs of imprisonment.

Bess had completed her redevelopment of Chatsworth by 1570. Mary was given apartments on the east wing of the house, above the Great Hall, but facing an inner courtyard for security. That summer, Elizabeth sent Cecil and other councillors to negotiate an agreement with Mary by which she would return to Scotland and retake the throne, sending her son, James, to England as a hostage. Mary was eager for the plan, but the Scots nobles, revelling in their freedom from royal authority and enjoying their customary feuds, refused to co-operate. Bess was stuck with her house-guest.

Mary's main focus of attention was plotting to have her marriage to Bothwell annulled, so that she could marry Norfolk, now released from the Tower. Unsurprisingly, the scheme, known as the Ridolfi Plot, was discovered and Bess watched Shrewsbury ride to London to preside over Norfolk's trial. Sir Ralph Sadler again journeyed to Sheffield to help Bess during her husband's absence. During this period, Mary was distressed to the point of illness at the failure of the plot, and Bess seldom left her.

Norfolk was condemned. Before Bess had the chance to break the news of his impending execution to Mary, the queen had already heard of it. Bess asked why she was weeping, and was told that *'her ladyship could not be ignorant of the cause'*. Mary went on to say that she was concerned that Norfolk would suffer for a letter she had recently written to Elizabeth. Bess replied that no letter of Mary's could possibly make any difference. Norfolk had been found guilty by his peers – chief amongst them her own husband. They would not have condemned him without clear proof.

From this point onward, Bess and Shrewsbury would be hard-pressed to keep up with Mary's efforts to regain her freedom.

Chapter 7: Family Arrangements

When Bess married Shrewsbury, unless their marriage agreement provided otherwise, he became the legal owner of all the property she held that was not already settled, by her or her previous husbands, on her children. The details of the actual settlement are not known, but in 1572, they were altered.

Shrewsbury agreed to settle all Bess' lands on her two younger sons, William and Charles, with Bess retaining a life interest.

The reason given in the deed was that the land grant was in consideration of Shrewsbury's considerable debts to his wife, the sums he had agreed previously to pay to his step-sons and to discharge his responsibility for some of Bess' own debts, although we do not know what those liabilities were. Unusually, the deed was not witnessed, just signed by Shrewsbury, which led to trouble later. In 1572, however, Bess and Shrewsbury were still on excellent terms.

1572 brought more political problems. The Massacre of St Bartholomew in Paris caused outrage, and Elizabeth sent orders for Mary to be even more heavily guarded – even a short move from Sheffield Castle to the manor house was not permitted. Later though, she was permitted to take the waters at Buxton in a house that Shrewsbury, at some expense, had had built in the newly-fashionable spa town. It is not clear whether Bess was part of the party. She may have taken the opportunity to visit Chatsworth, which is in close proximity.

During the early 1570s, Henry Cavendish returned home and set up his household with Grace at Tutbury Abbey. Soon, both he and Charles were proving to be less than satisfactory sons. Two of Henry's men became involved in a brawl in which one was killed, and Henry himself became involved in a similar fatal contretemps, leading to investigation by the Privy Council.

Charles provoked a letter from Shrewsbury to Bess in which he asked her to keep her son under control – he and his friends had gone out poaching one night.

By 1574, Bess had only one unmarried child. Elizabeth Cavendish was nineteen – somewhat late for a marriage to be agreed. There had been one negotiation, with the husband of Bess' old friend, Katherine, Duchess of Suffolk, Richard Bertie. Bertie had suggested their son, Peregrine, who was heir to Katherine's barony of Willoughby de Ereseby. Nothing had come of the discussions, perhaps because Bess knew that Queen Elizabeth disliked Katherine, and had refused ever to receive her at court. What would be the point of marrying her daughter to a mere baron, who was not favoured by the queen?

Nevertheless, Bess and Katherine remained friends, and the Dowager Duchess visited Chatsworth in 1574, which annoyed the queen, although she could hardly complain about private visits. What Bess and Katherine actually discussed cannot be proven, but, not long after, Bess removed her household to Rufford Abbey, where she entertained Lady Margaret Douglas, Countess of Lennox.

Lady Lennox, who, despite being a Catholic, had been friends with Lady Suffolk since their time together as ladies-in-waiting to Queen Katherine Parr, was also the mother-in-law of the Queen of Scots. After her son, Darnley's, death, Lady Lennox had been bitter against Mary, accusing her of complicity in the murder and begging Queen Elizabeth to avenge her. By 1574, however, she had become convinced of Mary's innocence.

Although Elizabeth was apparently unaware of the rapprochement between Lady Lennox and Mary, she was nervous of any meeting between the two, so, when Lady Lennox received permission to travel to her northern estates, she was forbidden from going via Chatsworth or Sheffield Castle. Nothing had been said about Rufford Abbey, so Lady Lennox took the opportunity, after leaving Lady Suffolk at Grimsthorpe, to call on Lady Shrewsbury and her daughter, Elizabeth Cavendish.

It so happened that Lady Lennox was accompanied by her son, Lord Charles Stuart, Earl of Lennox, just the same age as Elizabeth Cavendish. Lord Lennox had a strong (although not uncontested) claim to be the heir to the crown of Scotland.

Lady Lennox had no sooner arrived at Rufford than she felt ill. Bess was so engaged with looking after her that the two ladies had no time to supervise their children, who promptly fell in love to such an unrestrained degree that they had to be speedily married – or so the ladies informed Cecil when Elizabeth found out. Nothing was said of the great advantage to Bess in allying herself to the royal family of Scotland, likely to be the royal family of England in due course, or to Lady Lennox of the Cavendish and Shrewsbury money that she desperately needed.

Elizabeth was in a quandary. She trusted Shrewsbury to guard the Queen of Scots, but now she had potentially to punish his wife for becoming mother-in-law to Queen Mary's own brother-in-law and cousin. However fond she had once been of Bess, she must have been cursing her name. Shrewsbury wrote to Cecil that, although the marriage had been canvassed between the two ladies the previous year, they had not though it important enough to trouble the queen with it – a disingenuous statement at best. The actual event had taken place without Shrewsbury's knowledge, but he hoped the queen would be her usual *'good and gracious'* self and not think of either Bess or himself as anything other than her Majesty's *'most true and faithful servants.'*

Chapter 8: Royal Wrath

The two countesses were immediately summoned to London. Lady Lennox, together with her son and new daughter-in-law, were put under house arrest at the Lennox house in Hackney, before Lady Lennox was conveyed to the Tower for the third time in her life. There is no evidence of Bess being sent to join her.

The Earl of Huntingdon was deputed to investigate the matter. Although Durant describes Huntingdon as *'impartial'*, and not a friend to any of the parties, he was probably warmly disposed towards Bess. His wife, Lady Katherine Dudley, was the daughter of the late Duke of Northumberland and had been part of the circle surrounding the Greys in the 1540s and 1550s, amongst whom Bess and William Cavendish had found their friends.

Shrewsbury wrote several letters to Burghley, attempting to exonerate himself from any suspicion – even suggesting a marriage with Burghley's daughter for his last unmarried son.

Burghley, never one to take risks, declined. He warned Shrewsbury that Elizabeth was beginning to suspect that he was too attached to Mary, and he himself had thought so when he had joined the bathing expedition at Buxton.

Elizabeth was so sensitive that when Shrewsbury wrote that his son Gilbert and Mary had had their first child, he received a reprimand from Elizabeth. No strangers should have been admitted to Sheffield Castle whilst Mary was there. Shrewsbury was obliged to write back that only a midwife had been allowed in. The baby had been christened by him with his other children.

The Lennox marriage, whatever its motivation, proved fruitful. In November 1575, a daughter, named Arbella, was born. This was yet another thorn in Elizabeth's side. Whilst many objected to Mary, Queen of Scots as heir on account of her religion, and her nationality, Arbella Stuart was born in the realm, was the great-great-grand-daughter of Henry VII, and would undoubtedly be brought up as a Protestant. If she had been a boy, she might well have been preferred to her cousin, James VI of Scotland.

In due course, Elizabeth recovered her temper and permitted Lady Lennox to leave the Tower and Bess to once again frequent the company of Queen Mary, seemingly accepting that the two countesses had not been masterminding a plot to displace her. Whilst Bess' gamble on Elizabeth Cavendish's marriage had partially paid off, the young Countess of Lennox was soon widowed when Charles died in 1577.

Queen Mary had confirmed his place in the Scottish succession, and had also signified her wish that Elizabeth Lennox be paid dower from the Lennox lands in Scotland, with Arbella to inherit the earldom. The Scots government entirely ignored Mary's wishes – which probably did not surprise Bess. She paid a visit to Queen Elizabeth, who was glad to see her, and wrote a letter in favour of Arbella's rights to the Regent Morton, however it was of no more use than Mary's letter had been – the Lennox title was bestowed on Arbella's elderly great-uncle.

It is unlikely Elizabeth had been enthusiastic in her pleas. An heir on her doorstep with land and income of her own, not dependent on Elizabeth or her English family, would have been destabilising for the queen. Bess and Lady Lennox, however, continued to treat the little girl as though she were a countess.

Because Elizabeth Cavendish had married without her step-father's consent, he refused to pay her dowry. She and her daughter were thus dependent on Lady Lennox, the majority of whose estates had been confiscated by the Crown. In 1575, Leicester stayed with Bess at Chatsworth, after taking the waters at Buxton. He agreed to ask Elizabeth for maintenance for Arbella, presumably out of the English Lennox lands, which was eventually granted.

Chapter 9: Financial Worries

Soon, money troubles began to raise their ugly heads. Shrewsbury was feeling the pinch of his guardianship of Mary. He had never received sufficient from the Crown to cover his costs, and in 1575, Elizabeth proposed reducing the money from the £52 per week agreed in 1569, to £30 per week on the pretext that Mary's household ought to have been drastically cut.

Love flew out the window as poverty came in the door. Shrewsbury, suffering from extremely painful gout, money worries and the stress of his position, began to be fractious and quarrelsome. His family feared his outbursts of temper and his relationship with Bess began to deteriorate. In the summer of 1577 they had a bitter quarrel when he asked her to dismiss a groom. She asked his reasons for wanting the man thrown out, but he would not give her a clear answer. In a time when there was no job market, dismissal was a serious step. Bess had a duty to her servants to look after them, if they served her well. By sacking him, she could be condemning him to severe hardship, and perhaps even punishment as a vagrant.

There was another argument about Bess' embroiderers and the argument over the groom was unresolved. Whilst Shrewsbury was at Bolsover, Bess left Sheffield Castle and went to Chatsworth. On being told by his son that she was absent, Shrewsbury repeated their quarrel to Gilbert, adding that Bess had '*scolded like one that came from the Bank*' (the South Bank in London, then famous for prostitution). He was angry, however, that she was not there to greet him. *'Is she so full of malice that she would not tarry one night for my coming?'*

Gilbert sought to bring his father to a more reasonable turn of mind, pointing out how much Bess loved him, and how upset she was over the quarrel. Shrewsbury agreed that she loved him, and emphasised how much he loved her in return. Gilbert then wrote to Bess, repeating the conversation and urging her to return. As an added inducement, he told her that his son, George, was thinking of her. Sadly, George would not see his grandmother again. He died, aged two, on 11th August 1577.

Bess was distraught by the child's death. Shrewsbury asked permission to go to her at Chatsworth, taking Mary with him as Bess was too upset to travel. So, at this period, we can conclude that, despite some arguments, the couple were still attached to each other.

There was soon another death to contend with. Margaret Lennox died in February 1578. She was buried in state at Westminster Abbey, with Bess amongst the mourners. Following the death of her son, Charles Lennox, Lady Lennox had been granted the wardship of Arbella. Shrewsbury swiftly wrote to Burghley, Master of the Court of Wards, requesting that the wardship remain in the family and Elizabeth Lennox was permitted to keep her child. If Shrewsbury had not obtained his request Arbella would have been separated from her mother. From the queen's point of view, it was probably better that this potential heir be in the safe hands of the Shrewsburys, rather than creating temptation for some perhaps less loyal noble. Additionally, Elizabeth was freed of the potential cost of maintaining a semi-royal child.

Bess wrote a letter of thanks when Shrewsbury's request was granted. But Elizabeth Lennox had no means of support. The Scots government would not allow her to receive dower from the Scottish lands – technically, they were within their rights as she had had no dowry, having married without her step-father's permission. At the same time, Elizabeth confiscated the rest of the English lands, allegedly to pay Margaret Lennox' debts. Even Margaret's jewels, which she had willed to Arbella, were lost, when they were stolen by her executor, Thomas Fowler, who took them to Scotland.

Eventually, Bess badgered Shrewsbury into a dowry of £3,000 for Elizabeth Lennox, but it was not released until after the young widow's death in 1582. Bess therefore took on the maintenance of her daughter and granddaughter, although she did squeeze £400 per annum out of the queen for Elizabeth, and a further £200 for Arbella. Although Queen Mary issued a warrant demanding the jewels from Fowler, which was ignored, she did not make any provision for the child from her French income.

It is from around this period that the painting of Arbella as a small child dates. The legend reads 'Countess of Lennox.'

Bess was invited to court that Christmas, with her daughter and Arbella, and spent considerable time with the queen. Lord Leicester wrote to Shrewsbury to tell him what a great favourite

Bess was at court and how her wisdom and noble bearing were admired.

Chapter 10: More Financial Affairs

By 1583, it became apparent that Henry and Grace Cavendish were unlikely to have children. Bess began to look on her second son, William, as her long-term heir. William, who had already been knighted, was altogether more satisfactory than Henry, who, although he had no legitimate children, was so busy that he became known as the *'common bull of Derbyshire and Staffordshire.'*

In 1583, Bess purchased the estate of late brother, James Hardwick of Hardwick Hall, for her second son. James had died bankrupt, and the estate was sold for £9,500. This was definitely not a bargain for Bess – the income was only £341. She may have overpaid for sentimental reasons, or to maintain family honour by enabling her brother's debts to be paid. Shrewsbury was unwilling, in Bess' view, or unable, in actual financial fact, to contribute.

Henry Cavendish was costing Shrewsbury a fortune, he had dowries to find for his daughters, his eldest son, Francis, was in debt, and the money to maintain Queen Mary was insufficient, and often late. Bess too, he complained, was pressing him for money.

He was talking of selling his plate (the usual method of storing gold or silver in a time before banks) and his share in a ship '*The Talbot*' which carried the produce from his northern estates to market in London, and even went on a few (unsuccessful) privateering ventures with Sir John Hawkins.

The earl had also over-extended himself with his new prodigy house, Worksop Manor. In the fashion of the time, he wished to escape from the dark, mediaeval castles he owned into something like Burghley House, Longleat, or, of course, Chatsworth. The Worksop project was one that Bess and her husband could share – although building projects then, as now, frequently ended in frustration and quarrels after delays and overruns.

These difficulties were compounded when a group of Shrewsbury's tenants in the Peak Forest walked to London to petition against enclosure of lands and increases in their rents. After the uprisings against enclosures of the 1540s, and the recent Rising of the Northern Earls, Elizabeth and her government tended to look sternly on enclosing (most of her ministers having done all they needed to in that regard many years before.) The tenants' petitions were therefore looked on favourably and the rents were lowered – an embarrassment for Shrewsbury, who felt slighted and unappreciated.

In 1581, Mary was causing more headaches. She had sustained an injury falling from her horse and the Privy Council, hearing her complaints of ill-health, and Shrewsbury's constant requests for more funds, sent Robert Beale to investigate the situation. Beale spent three weeks questioning the queen, Shrewsbury, Bess and everyone else he could think of.

Mary complained incessantly of her health, but Bess gave it as her opinion that the queen was exaggerating – the friendship the two women had shared had definitely cooled. Shrewsbury explained how much money he was losing each year. Beale's report resulted in some slight relaxation of Mary's imprisonment but Mary's own request that Shrewsbury receive the money owing to him was ignored.

Troubles came thick and fast. Early in 1582, Elizabeth Lennox died. In her will, she remembered her stepfather fondly, and committed her daughter to Bess' care. Shrewsbury wrote to Sir Francis Walsingham that Bess was taking her daughter's death *'grievously... she cannot think of aught but tears.'* Both Bess and Shrewsbury quickly requested Elizabeth to continue the £400 per annum allowance for Arbella. Their pleas fell on deaf ears. That summer, Bess' daughter-in-law, Margaret Kitson, wife of Charles, died just after bearing a son.

Later the same year, Shrewsbury's eldest son, Francis, died heirless and in debt. Giles was now Shrewsbury's heir, and the earl seemed to feel that Bess and her daughter Mary (Giles' wife) had been ghoulishly waiting for just this outcome. He disliked Mary because he felt she encouraged her husband to support Bess, rather than himself in their disputes.

As the threat from Spain increased in the early 1580s, the pressure to hunt out Catholics also grew. Elizabeth's original policy of asking no questions if the approved service were attended had not served to resolve matters. The seminary priests and Jesuits who were coming into England were evangelising and giving new strength to the old faith.

Derbyshire was full of Catholic families, many related to Bess – the Foljambes, the Babingtons, the Fitzherberts and the Pierrepoints among them. Whilst Bess herself was Protestant (although she does not seem to have been more than conventionally religious), she cannot have been comfortable with her husband's increased diligence in searching out Catholics who were old friends.

As Shrewsbury's money troubles became worse, Bess prospered. She acquired huge tracts of land for her sons in Derbyshire, retaining a life interest for herself. The origin of the capital for these purposes is unclear as her annual income from the lands under the settlement agreed with Shrewsbury in 1572 was only around £2,500. In addition to this life-interest in her sons' lands, she received an annual allowance from Shrewsbury of £800.

Chapter 11: Marital Disputes

By the end of 1579, it was common knowledge that the Shrewsburys were on bad terms. The queen became concerned about the security of Mary, in a household that was riven with strife. There was some rapprochement, perhaps in response to a hint dropped by Leicester about Elizabeth's displeasure, and in 1580 the earl was again addressing Bess as *'My own Sweetheart'*.

But the harmony did not last. What exactly was at the bottom of their quarrels is impossible to state with certainty – marital quarrels are not always about their apparent subject! Money was probably at the heart of it – Shrewsbury was in dire financial straits whilst Bess was prospering and still demanding he fulfil his monetary commitments to her and her children.

The stress of keeping Mary captive was probably close to unbearable – if she had escaped to raise an army, Shrewsbury would have been ruined, and all his family with him. It is also possible, looking at the whole pattern of Shrewsbury's behaviour that he had some illness that affected his mental capacity – perhaps stroke or dementia.

One of Bess' gentlewomen, Frances Buttrell, assigned the cause of the couple's unhappiness to the Queen of Scots. *'The cause of her Lord's hard dealing with her is that the Scottish Queen cannot abide her.'* How or why Bess and Mary came to fall out is unrecorded but, given the stresses and strains of being cooped up together, very human.

Shrewsbury was now very short of money – pleas to Elizabeth fell on deaf ears, and even Walsingham was unable to move the queen, although he hinted that if Shrewsbury had insufficient funds he might not be able to guard Mary properly. In a regime of economy the earl imposed, he stopped paying Bess all of her allowance.

In February 1583 Bess and Shrewsbury were still on good enough terms for them to write, separately, to Burghley and Elizabeth, requesting forgiveness for having arranged the marriage of Bess' nephew, John Wingfield, to Katherine Suffolk's widowed daughter, Susan, Countess of Kent. As neither individual was a member of the royal family, it is difficult to understand why Elizabeth should be angry about it.

In the summer of that year, Bess left Sheffield Castle for a trip to Chatsworth. She parted on good terms with her husband, who assured he would send for her within a few days. But he did not. It seems that although Bess had enormous freedom as a wife, she could not return to her husband's home without permission – although this may have been because of the presence of Mary. Perhaps Shrewsbury needed to give written consent to everyone who came to her place of imprisonment. At any rate, he never again gave permission for Bess to return, and ceased paying her annual allowance.

The family was divided – Gilbert supported his stepmother (also his mother-in-law), whilst Henry Cavendish supported Shrewsbury. The earl's younger sons, Henry and Edward Talbot, received instructions to stay away from Bess on their return from education in France, but they also bore a letter from Leicester, telling Shrewsbury to resolve his marital differences.

Shrewsbury had declared that the land agreement made with Bess was no longer valid. Under it, she was not entitled to sell land, but he claimed that she had done so. He therefore considered it void and attempted to take back control of all the lands that she had brought to the marriage. The tenants of the St Loe and Cavendish lands were told to pay their rents to the earl, not the countess, and systematic aggression was employed – including an attack on Chatsworth, resulting in smashed windows, and on Charles Cavendish's manor where the fences were torn down.

Shrewsbury himself, leading some forty mounted men, attacked Chatsworth. William Cavendish sought to hold him off with weapons, including a pistol, but Bess was forced to leave. She retreated to Hardwick, taking some of the furnishings of Chatsworth with her.

The earl made a formal complaint to the Privy Council, accusing Bess and her sons of robbery and armed resistance to authority. Orders came from the Council to the local Justices who sentenced William to imprisonment in the Fleet gaol.

There is no evidence of Bess stirring up trouble against her husband. Her letters suggest she wished to return to the marital home and resolve their differences, but Shrewsbury seems to have been suffering such mental stress at to become completely irrational.

Leicester, making another trip to the spa at Buxton, called to see Bess to hear her side of the story. She told him that

Shrewsbury was making accusations against her of wrong-doing but would not tell her exactly what she had done to offend him. As to the report Leicester had received that Bess had told Shrewsbury that she could harm him, if she wanted to, she denied it utterly. Leicester wrote to Shrewsbury, explaining that Bess wanted to return to him, and hinting that the earl had been unreasonable in forbidding Gilbert to visit his wife, Mary, who was with her mother, having just had another child.

Shrewsbury was clearly ill – he had strange swellings, agonising gout and had sudden outbursts of temper. Stress was killing him. It became even worse when rumours started to spread that he and Mary had had an affair, and that she had born at least one child by him. Who started the rumours is impossible to say: Queen Mary blamed William and Charles Cavendish (although not Bess). The English government certainly benefited from the rumours as they undermined Mary's latest plan to marry Philip of Spain. Shrewsbury accused Bess of manufacturing the tale.

The earl was completely unreasonable on the subject of his wife – accusing her of hatred and malice, of slandering him and using 'sinister practices' to dishonour him. He did not give any specifics, and the reaction of others suggests that they were astonished by his outbursts and treatment of the wife he had once loved.

Chapter 12: Vicious Rumour

The reason for Mary's change of heart towards Bess may have been resentment over the birth of Arbella. Mary told the French Ambassador that nothing had alienated her from Bess more than the countess' plan to have Arbella crowned. Mary was still hoping that she would inherit Elizabeth's throne, as she was some nine years younger than the English queen – or even grasp it through an uprising. If Elizabeth chose to nominate Arbella as her heir, then both Mary and her son would be cut out of the succession.

Bess was already looking for possible husbands for her granddaughter in the early 1580s. Leicester's son was one possibility, but there was doubt as to whether Elizabeth would permit it, and the idea was not broached with her. Mary wrote about this plan to the French ambassador, hoping he would cause trouble for Bess by repeating it to Elizabeth. Whether the match would have been allowed is moot as the prospective bridegroom died in 1584.

In his response to Shrewsbury's letter of condolence for his son's loss, Leicester urged his friend to make up his quarrel with Gilbert – he should treasure his son, not quarrel with him. In particular, he advised Shrewsbury not to try to persuade Gilbert to separate from his wife.

Queen Mary was, by now, extremely bitter against Bess. She wrote a long letter revealing (or inventing) unpleasant and defamatory remarks that she alleged Bess had made about Elizabeth – that she and Leicester were lovers, that the French envoy Simier, had enjoyed the queen's favours, that even two men were not enough to satisfy the queen's lust and so on. David Durant does not believe this letter was ever sent. If it had been, Elizabeth, although she might not have believed all of the allegations, would probably have assumed that Bess had, at the least, passed some derogatory remarks about her and been less supportive of her over the next few years.

Whether or not Elizabeth saw the letter, she certainly received Mary's and Shrewsbury's separate requests for an enquiry into the allegation that they were lovers. A hearing was convened for the summer of 1584.

Shrewsbury arranged for an interim gaoler (Sir Ralph Sadler), transported Mary to Wingfield Manor, and departed for the capital. Bess had already arrived in London by August. She wrote again to her husband, asking him to explain what she had done to wrong him, and entreating him to take her back into his favour. Shrewsbury arrived in London in September, by which time he found Bess had been well-received by the queen and council – an indication that Elizabeth had never been sent Mary's letter referred to above.

Bess and her sons came before the Council, and on bended knees denied either inventing or spreading the rumour about Mary and Shrewsbury. They also affirmed that, to their knowledge, Mary had not born a child since being in England.

Shrewsbury asked to be relieved of the burden of being Mary's gaoler, and Elizabeth and the Council could probably see the toll on his health, his finance, and his marriage when he was in front of them. He was permitted to handover responsibility to Sadler, who was then replaced by Sir Amyas Paulet. The final decision may have been precipitated by Shrewsbury allowing his brother-in-law, the Catholic Earl of Rutland, to visit Mary. Whilst Shrewsbury was above suspicion, his judgement was obviously declining.

Bess probably rejoiced at this news, perhaps believing that without Mary stirring trouble, she and her husband might be reconciled, but Shrewsbury had different ideas and sought a separation.

Chapter 13: Royal Commission

Queen Elizabeth, although not married herself, took a strict view of marital duty and harmony. She would have no truck with Shrewsbury's plans, but instituted a further inquiry into the state of the earl and countess' marriage. It took place in December 1584, presided over by Lord Chancellor Bromley and two Chief Justices. Each side was to put forward a case in writing and appoint Counsel.

Shrewsbury claimed, first, that the 1572 settlement was a forgery, then that he had misunderstood it, thinking it for Bess only, not for her sons, and added that Bess had badgered him into giving her money when he was ill. He thought that all the lands she had bought in truth belonged to him, as he had financed them.

Bess counter-claimed that the deed was valid and had allowed Shrewsbury to avoid paying out large cash sums to the Cavendish brothers that her original marriage settlement had required. She further stated that all the new lands had been bought by the brothers themselves, financed by borrowing. Whilst the investigation took place, Shrewsbury stayed at his manor in Chelsea, whilst Bess retired to Derbyshire.

The verdict of the Commission completely vindicated Bess. The 1572 document was accepted as genuine, all the Cavendish brothers' lands were confirmed to them, Shrewsbury had to return the rents he had wrongly gathered and welcome his wife back to his home. Bess was to pay Shrewsbury £500 per annum.

Shrewsbury had no option but to accept the verdict, although he told Leicester he thought it poor recompense for his years of service to the queen. Within weeks, however, he had changed his mind and refused to implement any of the Commission's instructions. He continued to harass the Cavendish tenants, refused to welcome Bess home, and would not pay over the missing rents. He wrote abusive letters to Bess, and a missive to the queen that lacked proper respect. Her Majesty and the Council concluded that he was mentally ill and treated him gently.

Nevertheless, Shrewsbury was left to continue a policy of repression against Bess' tenants and after one flagrant miscarriage of justice, the queen ordered a second Commission. This one took place at Wollaton and was presided over by Shrewsbury's brother-in-law, Sir John Manners, and Sir Frederick Willoughby, an old friend of Bess'. The same evidence was reviewed, and a similar result reached, although William Cavendish had to pay Shrewsbury for plate and furniture taken from Chatsworth.

Shrewsbury implemented some of the orders against him, but again refused a request from Bess to allow her back to his home. He accused her of influencing Burghley and Walsingham against him, and even suggested that the queen was prejudiced in Bess' favour. He vowed that he would not receive Bess into his house again.

Such flagrant abuse of royal authority could not be permitted. Shrewsbury was bound over in the eye-watering sum of £40,000 to take his wife back, and to perform the articles agreed by the first and second Commissions. By now, Bess was losing patience. When faced with the list of items taken by William but now demanded by Shrewsbury, she disputed every one of them. Whilst some were ridiculous – Shrewsbury claimed sheets from seventeen years before – she found an objection to each item. Clearly, she was no longer open to a true reconciliation either.

Within a few days of living in the same house, following Elizabeth's express command, the two were quarrelling again. Shrewsbury again accused Bess of some unspecified malice, to which she responded that she did not understand what she had done wrong.

Elizabeth and her Council were at their wits' end – it was not truly practicable to punish Shrewsbury by demanding the £40,000 bond, and he was also needed elsewhere. Mary, Queen of Scots had finally fallen into one of the traps laid for her and acquiesced at the assassination of Elizabeth. Shrewsbury, as Earl Marshal, was required to preside at her trial and execution. He had the terrible duty of signalling to the headsman to do his work.

It must have been a dreadful moment – the guarding of Mary had destroyed his peace, health and marriage, but to see her die at his command when he had known her for nearly twenty years was shocking and it was recorded that tears streamed down his face.

In the spring of 1587, Elizabeth forced another reconciliation between the couple. Shrewsbury complied at last, and he and Bess first took up married life again at Chelsea, and then at Wingfield. But it could not last. Shrewsbury left her at Wingfield and seldom returned, nor would he pay her expenses as required by the queen.

Shrewsbury found himself a new companion – Mrs Eleanor Britton. Probably Bess was relieved by this – and perhaps also hoped that Mrs Eleanor would give her troubled husband some peace, although she still petitioned to return to him herself, or at least to be allowed to visit him. Whilst the earl avoided his wife, he stopped harassing her tenants, so matters improved. Bess herself spent most of her time at Wingfield or at Hardwick.

During the years following the Armada of 1588, Arbella visited Elizabeth at court and was very well treated, but her position seems to have gone to her head a little (not surprising for a girl of thirteen or fourteen) and Elizabeth sent her back to Bess.

Whilst Bess' health continued to be excellent, Shrewsbury's deteriorated. In a brief moment of return to his former self, he sent a kind letter to his daughter-in-law Mary, after years of abuse, and also proved prescient when he predicted that the Lady Arbella would bring trouble on his house.

Shrewsbury died in November 1590 and was buried with all the honours of an Earl Marshal in the Church of St Peter and St Paul, Sheffield. Some 20,000 spectators watched the procession and around 8,000 received the funeral dole. His epitaph, designed by himself, makes no mention of his second wife.

Chapter 14: A Trip to London

Neither did Shrewsbury's will mention Bess. This would probably have been the case even if they had not quarrelled, as her dower would have been set at the time of her marriage. He appointed his younger sons, Henry and Edward, as executors, but they declined to act. Bess was suggested by the supervisors (Burghley) as executrix, Gilbert, now 6th Earl of Shrewsbury, rejected the idea and took responsibility for the will.

Gilbert had taken Bess' part in all disputes with her husband, and was a fond husband to Bess' daughter, but now their relationship changed completely. To his utter astonishment, never having believed his father's complaints of poverty, Gilbert was saddled with debts – his brother Francis had left debts, Shrewsbury had left debts, and Mrs Eleanor had stripped Sheffield of plate and jewels.

Initially, Bess tried to come to an accommodation with Gilbert about her dower rights, but, after he failed to observe two agreements, she was disinclined to come to a third. She was persuaded into a final agreement, to be paid on 31st March 1591, but when it was not honoured, felt she had little choice but to pursue the matter in court.

Whilst Bess was asking for less than her due, it was only three months since Shrewsbury's death, and it is hard to escape the feeling that Bess was putting money above family feeling. She had an excellent income already, and whilst her dower rights amounted to some £3,000 per annum, she could probably have afforded to wait whilst Gilbert sorted the estate out.

Perhaps her mother's experiences of financial hardship had had a life-long effect on Bess, who prized financial security above almost everything. She managed her estates exceptionally efficiently – each had to pay its way, and she demanded all her legal rights. At the same time, she fulfilled her obligations properly and was a fair landlord to her tenants. She lent money to her neighbours who were less thrifty, but did not hesitate to take up the security if they failed to pay.

An example of this firm grip on finances occurred in 1592. Bess' friend, Sir Francis Willoughby, had fallen into debt over the construction of Wollaton Hall. Bess lent £3,050 at 10% interest and security of lands to be held by Arbella during the period of the loan. After Sir Francis' death, the mortgage fell into arrears. A request to redeem it with full payment plus a year's interest was rejected as outside the strict period of redemption permitted in the agreement. At a stroke, Arbella now owned £15,000 worth of lands.

Bess wanted every penny she was entitled to after Shrewsbury's death, as she had now embarked on the greatest building project of her life – the new Hardwick Hall. She had made considerable improvements to the old hall that she had been born in, but the new building was to be one of the greatest architectural masterpieces of the whole era.

Whilst work was continuing on this sumptuous palace, fit for the grandmother of a girl who might one day be Queen of England, Bess took Arbella to court. The sixteen year old had been the subject of interest from the Duke of Parma as a potential bride for his son.

The trip to London was conducted almost as a royal progress. Bess and Arbella travelled in a coach, followed by William and Charles Cavendish and their wives (Charles had remarried), as well as Bess' gentlewomen. Some forty servants were necessary to look after them all in a journey that took a week. Reinforcing the image of Arbella as a possible queen, 40 shillings was doled out to the poor in each town they passed through.

The family took up residence at Shrewsbury House in Chelsea, where they stayed until July 1592. Huge sums of money were spent on outfitting Arbella for court, and on Bess' own wardrobe of sumptuous black gowns. Portraits of Arbella were painted for dispatch to Parma.

Bess was on good terms with the queen and attended her frequently during the visit. Although it has been claimed that the two quarrelled, other than the period of suspicion following the marriage of Elizabeth Cavendish to Charles Lennox, there is no evidence that Elizabeth ever treated Bess less than kindly and had supported her steadfastly against Shrewsbury's accusations.

Leicester, Hatton and Walsingham were now dead, and Burghley semi-retired so Bess needed to cultivate friends amongst the new circle surrounding the queen. She corresponded with Raleigh, Essex and Sir Robert Cecil, amongst others, hoping to build up support for Arbella's position. She received friends, both old and new, and gave generous hospitality, gifts and tips to high and low. In all, Bess spent over £6,300 during the time in London.

It was not all junketing – Bess was also trying her hardest to make sure that Gilbert could not bring any suit against her in London. If matters were heard in Derbyshire, she could probably influence the outcome.

Plague returned to London in the summer of 1592. The court was broken up as Elizabeth travelled to the West Country, and Bess and Arbella returned to Derbyshire. Nothing had been resolved about the marriage with Parma.

Chapter 15: Hardwick

Bess now threw herself into the works at Hardwick. She lived in the Old Hall with Sir William and his wife, but spent many hours overseeing the works, and checking the details of the weekly accounts. The stone, the timber, the iron and the marble all came from her estates, and she even set up a glass making plant on site.

Into this busy life crept danger. Burghley wrote that he had heard of a plot by Jesuits to abduct Arbella and take her to Flanders. Bess' suspicions immediately fell on Arbella's tutor, Mr Morley. Morley had previously asked Arbella for lands of £40 value, claiming that he had lost money by leaving Cambridge to become her tutor. Arbella refused, and referred him to her grandmother. He then said that he would stay with Arbella without any pay at all. Bess, ever the business woman, thought this so strange that she considered he must be up to no good, although she could not honestly say she had scented '*papistry*.'

Bess now felt that Arbella needed to be carefully watched – not for any fault in her, but because she might attract treasonable behaviour. Soon, the girl was almost as closely watched as Queen Mary had been. Bess was usually with her, no unknown guests came to the house and she could only walk or ride with constant attendance. It must have driven the poor girl almost to distraction.

For Bess, these were good years. She had her family about her, they celebrated all the traditional holidays in fine style, with copious food, parties and entertainments. She gave generous presents to all of her children and grandchildren and was affectionate to them all. Nevertheless, for her family she was probably a very controlling and dominating personality.

But feuds and arguments continued in the wider family. Gilbert, supported by Charles Cavendish, quarrelled with Sir John Stanhope. Stanhope had once been Gilbert's friend, as his father had been friend to Bess and Shrewsbury, but Gilbert accused him of betraying his trust. The matter escalated to brawls between their servants and even a duel (although not completed) between Charles and Stanhope. The queen was displeased. She did not like her courtiers to quarrel. The queen was inclined to blame Gilbert's wife, Mary, whom she thought led her husband in everything – much as his father had once believed.

Gilbert and Bess were still in dispute over her dower rights, and she felt obliged to appeal to the Privy Council. Gilbert was soon reviling her as his father had done. He was also quarrelling with his brother Edward, whom he accused of trying to poison him. Mary Shrewsbury was implicated in the affair, and called before the Master of the Rolls, although no action was taken. Gilbert and Mary were estranged from Bess, and deep in debt.

Matters improved slightly when in 1596, after a visit from Elizabeth's favourite, the Earl of Essex, Arbella was invited to court. Bess remained in Derbyshire, allowing Gilbert and Mary to chaperone their niece. Gilbert was sent on an official mission to

France, which he conducted successfully, but Mary put her satin-shod foot in it by requesting Elizabeth to allow her own daughters to be appointed as *'maids-of-honour'* to Arbella. Elizabeth responded that only royalty had maids-of-honour and Lord and Lady Shrewsbury could take themselves and their niece back to the country.

In October 1597, Bess finally moved into Hardwick Hall, accompanied by Arbella. Arbella's life was that of a doll in a gilded cage. There was no more talk of marriage for her, her bed was in her grandmother's room, and although she had every luxury and the house was full of companions, her life had little purpose. Bess meanwhile was still involving herself in business ventures, buying land (never selling) and giving mortgages in return for solid security.

As the 1590s progressed, more of Bess' family and friends died - including her daughter-in-law, Anne, William's wife, and three of her six children, and Lord Burghley, whom she had known for forty years. Equally distressing was an attack on Charles by the Stanhopes. Charles was shot and knifed, and although he survived the attack, a bullet lodged in his thigh, which could never be removed, despite the best efforts of the queen's own surgeons.

In 1601, Essex, who had been a friend of Arbella's, and might have been glad to see her as queen, was executed. Perhaps this reminder of death spurred Bess to commissioning her tomb and making her will.

Henry had had Chatsworth entailed upon him by his father, and Bess left him many of the contents. William received the vast majority of her wealth, with a bequest for Frances and Arbella. Gilbert, Mary, and rather unkindly, Charles, were completely cut out for their '*unkindness*' to her, although she did forgive them and leave them her blessing. This will, witnessed by eighteen people, was accompanied by a detailed inventory. Bess had been somewhat premature. She continued in good health for years to come.

Chapter 16: Last Years

Arbella was becoming increasingly unhappy and frustrated, seeing Bess as her gaoler. She hatched a plot to escape by marriage, choosing Edward Seymour, grandson of Lady Katherine Grey and Edward, Earl of Hertford. This was a phenomenally risky endeavour. Seymour had a claim to the throne. Partnered with Arbella, there was a realistic prospect of them being preferred to King James. Elizabeth would have no discussion of the succession, and severely punished any attempts to agree it.

A complex scheme was concocted to send the proposal to Lord Hertford. He was horrified when he received the message from Arbella and immediately reported it to the queen and council. A messenger was sent hot-foot to Hardwick. Arbella confessed, and

Bess was beside herself with fear and anger, although she had been assured that Elizabeth held her completely uninvolved.

Bess asked Elizabeth to either send Arbella to somewhere she could be kept safely, or allow her to be married. The queen rejected both requests, and in fact, thought that Arbella could be kept less strictly. Arbella's own plea to the queen to be allowed to come to court was also rejected.

Grandmother and granddaughter were effectively estranged. Arbella came up with another impractical scheme to escape, aided and abetted by the man Bess referred to as '*my bad son, Henry.*' This too, came to nothing.

More letters to Elizabeth were effectively pointless, as, in the spring of 1603, the queen, depressed at the death of her cousin and friend, Katherine, Lady Nottingham, succumbed to a throat infection and died, at the age of sixty-nine.

It was the end of an era, and Bess probably sincerely mourned the woman she had known for over fifty years, who had stood godmother to her son, and who had supported her through her difficult marriage to Shrewsbury.

Whatever hopes there might have been for Arbella were dashed. James VI succeeded as James I of England without incident. He bestowed his favour on Gilbert and Mary by staying with them at Worksop Manor on his journey south, which must have pleased Bess, even though she and they were estranged. He also signified his willingness to receive Arbella, and arranged for her to live with Henry Grey, Earl of Kent, and his wife at Wrest Park, Bedford.

The departure of Arbella was probably simultaneously a relief and a grief to Bess.

Arbella soon joined the court, but found herself short of money. Bess was not inclined to help her, any more than she agreed to help her son, Henry, even when requested to do so by Robert Cecil, now James' chief minister.

In 1605, Bess fell ill, and Arbella obtained leave to visit her. There was the show of reconciliation between them, but Bess found it hard to forgive her granddaughter for her perceived lack of gratitude. This lack of family kindness continued, when Gilbert presented yet another suit against his stepmother, which Bess, accustomed to defending suits, and always scrupulous in observing the rules, won. However, it did not make relations any easier.

Similarly, whilst she would give Henry small presents when he visited, she would not clear his debts.

As Bess approached her late seventies, she was estranged from three of her children, all of whom would have welcomed reconciliation, whether from genuine affection or for pecuniary motives. Charles was solvent, so his wish to be on good terms with her was probably genuine – and the quarrel had only come about because of his support for Gilbert. A slight thaw occurred when Gilbert and Mary's daughter, Lady Alathea Talbot, married the Earl of Arundel – the highest ranking earl in England.

Gradually, Bess and Mary Shrewsbury were reconciled, although Mary's leanings towards Catholicism were anathema to her mother. Bess had always remained on good terms with the Shrewsbury's children, and in late 1607, Gilbert and Mary were finally accepted as visitors again.

Bess may have felt mortality drawing on. Shortly after the visit, she took to her bed in the cold of an exceptionally severe winter. William, always the most dutiful, if the least interesting of her sons, sat by her bed and noted down her last requests. Frances and Charles visited her, and she wept for joy at seeing them. She made a verbal bequest of £4,000 to Charles, for land for his children and 2,000 marks for Frances.

On 13th February, 1608, Bess died. She had outlived her first husband by over sixty years, her second by fifty, her third by forty, and her last by seventeen. She had been born the daughter of a country gentleman, little richer than many yeoman, and died the richest woman in England, with her granddaughter a member of the royal family. Despite many quarrels and upsets, she had lived a life with much love and friendship and was respected and honoured by all her knew her.

She was buried with great ceremony, in the Church of All Saints, Derby.

Part 2: Aspects of Bess of Hardwick's Life

Chapter 17: Following the Footsteps of Bess of Hardwick

Like most Tudor women, Bess never left England, but she travelled regularly between her native Derbyshire and London, and to the estates of her third husband in Somerset, as well as with the court. Many of her later journeys related to supervision of her magnificent constructions at Chatsworth and Hardwick.

The numbers in the article below correspond to those on the map which follows.

*

Bess was born into a comfortable, but not grand, farmhouse called Hardwick Hall (1), just on the Derbyshire side of the county border with Nottingham. Although her father died when she was a child, leaving a minor heir, Bess' mother managed to retain the house for the younger siblings to live in. Mrs Hardwick remarried and had three more children, which probably made for a lively childhood. In later life, Bess lent money to her brother, James, secured on the Hardwick estate. When he died, a bankrupt, she bought out his other creditors. In 1587 she began a major refurbishment programme. The remains of this, known as Hardwick Old Hall, are in the care of English Heritage.

But the Old Hall was not enough for Bess' status as a countess. In 1590, a whole new hall was begun, based on designs by Robert Smythson, the most important architect of Elizabethan England. He worked on Longleat, and probably on Burghley House as well. These great 'prodigy houses' were symbols of wealth and power, built to last.

The majority of the building materials for Hardwick came from Bess' own land. She even built a glass factory, to create the magnificent *Hardwick Hall, more glass than wall*.

Today, Hardwick can be reached from Junction 29 of the M1, or from the A617 Chesterfield to Mansfield road.

Bess left her childhood home when she was about twelve, to enter the household of Anne, Lady Zouche at Codnor Castle (2). Lady Zouche had been a maid-of-honour to Queen Anne Boleyn, so this would have been a great opportunity for Bess. In fact, there is no hard evidence of Bess being in the Zouche household, but circumstantial information has led her biographers to think it probable.

Codnor Castle was one of the great mediaeval castles of England. Originally owned by the de Grey family, ownership fell into abeyance in 1496 between various branches of the family. Henry VII purchased the castle from the heirs for his son, Henry, Duke of York, later Henry VIII. When he became king, Henry VIII sold it back to Lord Zouche, one of the heirs of de Grey.

In 1634, the castle was sold and largely dismantled. The ruins are in the hands of the Codnor Castle Heritage Trust, which is hoping to protect them from further deterioration. Bess probably lived at Codnor from about 1539 – 1543. It is the likely location for her meeting with her first husband, Robert Barlow, although, as the Barlows were another Derbyshire family, she may already have known him.

Bess was widowed before her husband came into his inheritance, and disputes over her dower meant that she was once again obliged to earn her living. She was employed in the household of Lady Frances Grey (nee Brandon), Marchioness of Dorset at Bradgate (3), in Leicestershire.

This was a huge step up for Bess – Lady Dorset was the King's niece, and, whilst Henry had little time for her husband, Henry Grey, Marquess of Dorset, the two were still prominent in court circles. Like Bess' first employer, Lady Zouche, the Dorsets were religious reformers. Bess quickly became close to the whole family – all her life, she treasured an agate ring that Lady Dorset gave her, and a picture of the Dorset's oldest daughter, the luckless Lady Jane Grey.

Bradgate has been enclosed parkland for well over 800 years. The house that Bess lived in with the Dorsets was planned by Sir Thomas Grey, 1st Marquess of Dorset, the half-brother of Queen Elizabeth of York. The actual building work was done by his son, the 2nd Marquess, and completed around 1520. It was constructed of the fashionable, and extremely expensive, red brick.

It was at Bradgate that Bess met and married her second husband, Sir William Cavendish. He was considerably older than her, with two previous marriages behind him and at least two living daughters, but nevertheless, the couple soon developed a close working partnership that speedily increased their joint wealth. Bradgate descended in the Grey family, who continued to live in it for another two hundred years after the mid-sixteenth century. After 1739, it was replaced with a new house, and fell into ruin. These ruins can be viewed today – they are in the care of the Bradgate Park Trust, which also looks after the extensive woodlands. It can be reached by taking the A50 from Junction 22 of the M1.

After they were married, Bess and Cavendish lived mainly in London, in a house near St Paul's, and also at an estate called Northaw (4). Northaw village remains – tucked into the Hertfordshire countryside, just north of the M25. The manor of Northaw was originally a possession of the Abbey of St Albans. At the Dissolution of the Monasteries, it was granted to William Cavendish and his then wife, Margaret.

In 1552, Cavendish and Bess exchanged the manor, together with all their lands outside Derbyshire, for a large parcel of crown lands in their home county. It is suggested by Bess' biographer, David Durant, that the exchange was made in case a change of government resulted in questions about the status of former monastic lands. There is no trace today of the Cavendishes' home, and even the church dates only from the nineteenth century.

William Cavendish was probably originally from Cavendish, in Suffolk, but he was a younger son, so had no inheritance there. He and Bess were happy to acquire lands in Derbyshire. The manor of Chatsworth (5) was in the hands of the Leche family, probably relatives of Bess' mother, whose name was Elizabeth Leake (a homonym) and who married, as her second husband, Ralph Leche. When Ralph Leche's nephew, Francis, died without heirs, it provided an excellent opportunity for William and Bess to buy the estate. It was subsequently augmented after the sale of Northaw, as noted above.

Bess and Cavendish clearly had a vision of founding a great dynasty, in which they proved remarkably successful. To achieve the status they dreamed of, a great house was an important part of the visible success they needed to show. They began to build at Chatsworth, and this would prove to be one of the most rewarding projects of Bess' life. She spent many years improving and beautifying the house – perhaps in hopes of a visit from Queen Elizabeth.

Whilst Elizabeth never did visit, her favourite, the Earl of Leicester did, and Mary Queen of Scots was held there from time to time, when other locations needed to be cleaned.

Chatsworth was entailed on her eldest son, Henry Cavendish, but Bess retained a life-interest in it and spent a good deal of time there, particularly after she and her fourth husband became estranged. The current Chatsworth House, one of the greatest of all England's 'Stately Homes' has almost obliterated Bess' house, although it is built around the original courtyard plan she designed. The house is still the home of Bess and William's descendants, the Dukes of Devonshire.

Of course, such an ambitious couple as Bess and Cavendish could not spend all their time in Derbyshire. William was frequently in London, and in 1555, he arranged to rent a house at Brentford (6), from Sir John Thynne, where Bess could spend the winter with him. She was expecting her sixth child and did not like to be parted from her husband. Thynne proved to be a good friend to Bess. When Cavendish died in 1557 and was accused of peculation of Crown funds, he helped her both by leasing the Brentford house to her again, and arguing against a bill in Parliament that would have bankrupted the widow.

The Brentford Manor that Bess knew was replaced in 1628 by a truly delightful Jacobean house – well worth seeing.

Sir William Cavendish was buried in the Church of St Botolph-without-Aldersgate (8), near his mother and his first wife. A church was first built on the site in the twelfth century, and it received extensive improvements in the 1570s under Lord Mayor, Sir William Allen, who was born in the parish. By 1725, it was in such poor condition that it was demolished and rebuilt in the style of Wren. The structure was badly damaged by an IRA bomb in 1993, but repaired. A number of prominent late sixteenth century figures were buried here, including Lady Mary Keyes (née Grey), daughter of Bess' friend Frances, Duchess of Suffolk.

When Bess married Sir William St Loe in 1559, the couple became embroiled in a long-running dispute with St Loe's brother and sister-in-law, Edward and Margaret St Loe. The nub of the matter was the status of Sutton Court (7), in the curiously named village of Chew Magna, Somerset. When Bess first visited, perhaps thinking that she and St Loe would live there, she ordered various improvement works to the early fifteenth century house. In the event, Sutton was awarded after St Loe's death to Margaret St Loe for her lifetime, and Bess did not return.

Sutton Court was extensively rebuilt in the 1850s, and then converted in the late twentieth century to flats.

Like Sir William Cavendish, Sir William St Loe was also buried in London, but his resting place was Great St Helen's Church, Bishopsgate, London (9), alongside his father. This church was once attached to a Benedictine convent, but, after the house was dissolved in 1538, it became the parish church. St Helen's too, was severely damaged first by a bomb in 1992, and then by the 1993 bomb, which also killed three people. It has now been restored.

On her marriage to Shrewsbury, Bess' chief marital home became Sheffield Castle (10). The castle was at the heart of the settlement that grew up around the rivers Don and Sheaf, in Yorkshire. A timber structure was first erected in around 1100, which was burnt by Simon de Montfort in his rebellion against Henry III. It was rebuilt around 1270, and the owner, Thomas de Furnival, received a licence to crenellate the new stone structure. The castle came into the hands of the Talbot family when Maud Neville, 6th Baroness Furnivall, married John Talbot, who was created Earl of Shrewsbury in 1442. He is the *'Old Talbot'* of *Henry VI*.

The first Earl instigated wide-ranging repairs to the castle, which had two courtyards, with the usual range of buildings –

tower, hall, chapel, bakehouse etc. When Bess' husband, the 6th Earl, died, the castle, along with the Barony of Furnivall, passed to her step-son, Gilbert Talbot, 7th Earl, who was also her son-in-law. Gilbert and his wife, Mary Cavendish, only had daughters, so the Barony of Furnival fell into abeyance between their three daughters. Sheffield passed with Alathea Talbot to the Howard earls of Arundel. It fell to Parliament in the Civil War and was eventually slighted.

The site is now largely covered with other buildings, but a small portion of the remains can be seen below the Castle Market, by prior arrangement. The Friends of Sheffield Castle promote the archaeological investigation of the site.

It was largely at Sheffield that Mary, Queen of Scots was kept, although initially she was taken to one of Shrewsbury's other manors – Tutbury Castle (11), on the Derbyshire/Staffordshire border. Tutbury, once owned by John of Gaunt, Duke of Lancaster, was, by the mid-sixteenth century, damp, badly drained and completely unsuitable for a queen. Shrewsbury was also concerned that the local inhabitants were *'corrupted with Popery.'*

The castle's strong point was its defensibility. Bess was at Tutbury from time to time during the period of Mary's captivity – when the Queen first arrived in early 1569, Bess had had to furnish the place quickly by sending some of her own household goods from Sheffield Castle. Today, the ruins of Tutbury Castle, which can be visited by the public, are looked after by a trust.

Another of Mary, Queen of Scots' prisons was the Shrewsbury manor of Wingfield (12), near Alfreton, Derbyshire. Dating from the mid-15th century, the house was purchased by the 2nd Earl of Shrewsbury in 1456 on the death of its builder, Ralph, Baron Cromwell. Mary was kept there in 1569, and again in 1584 and 1585. It was at the centre of the Babington Plot, in which Sir Anthony Babington, a member of a prominent Derbyshire family well-known to Bess, attempted to hatch a plan to rescue the imprisoned queen.

Wingfield was damaged during the Civil War, after which it was sold to Immanuel Halton, who stripped away much of its stone and other materials to build a new house. This was abandoned in the late eighteenth century.

The ruins of Wingfield are cared for by English Heritage, but can only be visited by pre-booking.

Another of the great houses that Shrewsbury and Bess owned was Rufford Abbey (13). Rufford, once a Cistercian house, was acquired by Shrewsbury following the Dissolution of the Monasteries. Located in Nottinghamshire, it was a convenient place for Bess to meet Margaret, Lady Lennox, who had been forbidden from travelling within 30 miles of Mary, Queen of Scots. There, whilst Lady Lennox was being nursed by Bess, having been struck down by a convenient sickness, the two encouraged the speedy marriage of their children, Lord Charles Stuart, and Elizabeth Cavendish, incurring the wrath of Elizabeth I.

Shrewsbury and Bess extended the twelfth century property significantly, and it passed to their joint grand-daughter, Lady Mary Talbot. The Elizabethan house was transformed in the late seventeenth century, and today is in the care of English Heritage and Nottinghamshire County Council.

Of course, a wealthy couple like Bess and Shrewsbury needed a town house in London. They owned Shrewsbury House (14) in Chelsea. The exact location of the property is uncertain, but it was probably near Cheyne Walk. There are records of George Talbot, 4th Earl, and Francis, 5th Earl, staying at Shrewsbury House during Henry VIII's and Edward VI's reigns respectively. It was at Shrewsbury House that Bess and Shrewsbury effected some sort of reconciliation on Queen Elizabeth's orders in 1586, after which she was ordered to reside at Wingfield where she largely remained until after Shrewsbury's death.

Bess retained Shrewsbury House, presumably as part of the marriage settlement, and it passed to her son, William Cavendish. He was created Earl of Devonshire, and Shrewsbury House became attached to the earldom until it was sold in 1643. It was demolished in 1813.

The Earl of Shrewsbury died in 1590 and was buried in the Church of St Peter's in Sheffield, now known as Sheffield Cathedral. The origins of the church probably date to around the same time as Sheffield Castle, with additions and demolitions taking place over the centuries. The Talbot Chapel contains not just Bess' husband, but other members of the family. Shrewsbury's tomb has a model of both his wives on it, but, whilst his first wife, Lady Gertrude Manners, is buried with him, Bess is not. Despite her figure being on the tomb, the epitaph omits all mention of her.

For unknown reasons, Bess chose to be buried in All Saints (Allhallows as it was called then) Church (15), Derby, now the Cathedral, rather than beside any of her husbands, or her father, who was buried at the church local to Hardwick, Ault Hutnall, and where she had been baptised.

Bess began the design and construction of her impressive tomb during her lifetime, but directed that her funeral *'be not oversumptuous, or otherwise performed with too much vain and idle charge.'* Despite this, she left £2,000 to cover the costs. She was interred on 4th May 1608 following a sermon oration by the Archbishop of York. Above the vault, is a life-sized monument and a plaque on the wall commemorates her (although it dates from the time of her grandson, the Duke of Newcastle). The vault houses more than three dozen of Bess' Cavendish descendants.

The list below corresponds to the map which follows of places Bess would have known.

Key to Map

1. Hardwick Hall, Derbyshire
2. Codnor Castle, Derbyshire
3. Bradgate Park, Leicestershire
4. Northaw, Hertfordshire
5. Chatsworth, Derbyshire
6. Brentford House, London
7. Sutton Court, Chew Magna, Somerset
8. St Botolphs Church, London
9. Great St. Helens Church, London
10. Sheffield Castle, Yorkshire
11. Tutbury Castle, Burton-on-Trent, Staffordshire
12. Wingfield Manor, Alfreton, Derbyshire
13. Rufford Abbey, Ollerton, Nottinghamshire
14. Shrewsbury House, Chelsea, London
15. All Saints Church, Derby

Map

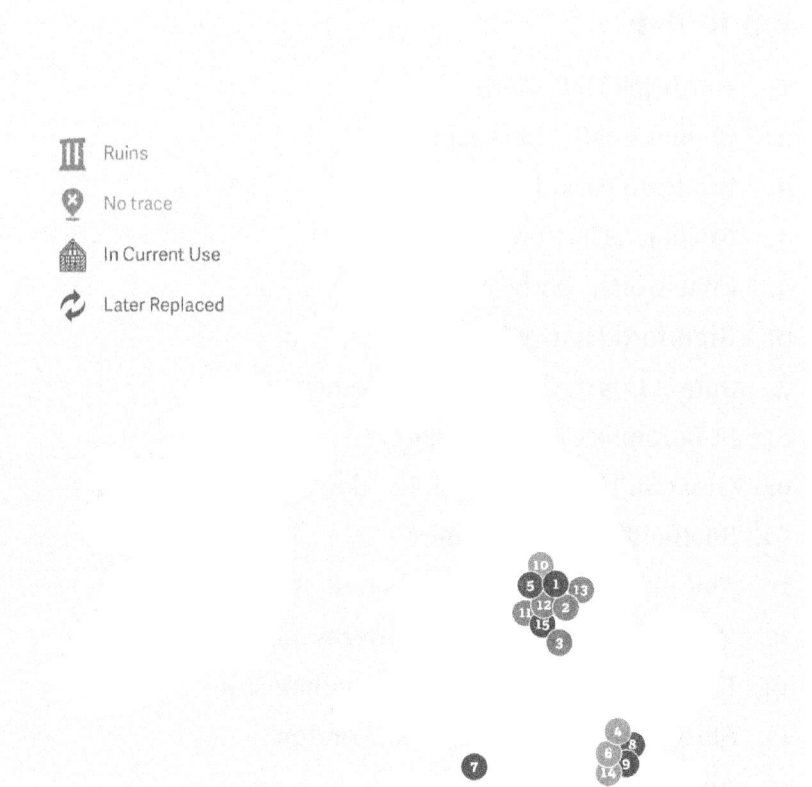

- Ruins
- No trace
- In Current Use
- Later Replaced

Chapter 18: Bess the Networker

'Networking' seems a very 2st century idea, conjuring up images of executives working a room, handing out business cards and treating strangers like long-lost friends – but the reality is that networking has underpinned political and business life since the dawn of civilization. Read any history of ancient Egypt, Rome, Greece or China and it will immediately become clear that who you knew was far more important than what you knew.

It was no different in the fifteenth, sixteenth and seventeenth centuries. To get ahead, you needed to build connections, in a system referred to in the earlier part of the period as *'good lordship'*. You would write to someone more important, or more influential than yourself, preferably someone with a remote blood relationship, give them a present – food, hunting dogs, gloves – explain what you needed and ask the person to be *'good lord'* or *'good lady'* to you. In due course, when your *'good lord'* wanted something in return – support in battle, putting in good word with the king, a job for a connection, or a land exchange, you were expected to return the favour.

These networks of reciprocal obligation were enhanced by the complex web of family relationships across the nobility and the gentry. Within the ruling class, from the senior nobles, right down to country gentry who seldom attended the court, marriages were used to cement an alliance, or settle disputes.

Because there was so much intermarriage, it often transpired that families found themselves on different sides of a dispute, because of more important or valuable obligations to others. The Wars of the Roses exemplify this – sisters would often find their husbands in conflict, and brothers would sometimes be on opposing sides. During the sixteenth century, the fault line of religion broke families apart. The Throckmorton family produced both confirmed Protestants, such as Elizabeth (Bess) who married Sir Walter Raleigh, and a Catholic branch involved in the Gunpowder Plot. In these circumstances, long-standing networks and connections of '*good lordship*' were often invoked to help the political loser out of a tricky corner.

So, in an age of political complexity and danger, keeping on good terms with your friends, relatives and connections was an integral component of a successful career – and there was no better networker than Elizabeth (Bess) Hardwick, who used what we might call her '*people-skills*' to build a career that took her from minor Derbyshire gentry, to the richest woman in England, after the queen.

*

Bess took her first steps on the Tudor career ladder in about 1540, when she was anything between 13 and 19 years old. Kinship ties had been invoked and Bess was accepted into the household of a distant cousin, that of George, Lord Zouche of Codnor, as attendant to his wife. Lady Zouche (née Anne Gainsford) in her youth had been attendant on Queen Anne Boleyn and is credited with introducing the queen to the work of

William Tyndale. This influence may account for Bess' firm Protestantism, despite Derbyshire generally being conservative in religion.

There are no direct records of Bess' time in the Zouche household, or whether she visited the court during that period, but her later network of friends and acquaintances suggest that she did. Bess was briefly married during 1543 – 45 to Robert Barlow, whose early death left Bess in financial difficulties. Until she won a court case for her dower rights in 1553, she needed to find financial support elsewhere. Her own family were in financial difficulties, so it was probably the need to find a home and income that took her into the household of Frances, Marchioness of Dorset, niece of King Henry VIII.

The Marquis, Henry Grey, was strongly evangelical in his views, and this like-mindedness in religion may have made Bess a good fit with the household at the time. Lady Zouche had a family connection to the marquis, as they were both descended from the Woodville family, but it was not close and they may not have been aware of it – on the other hand, it may have been strong enough for the marquis to take a recommendation as to Bess' suitability.

Bess now connected with a group of people who would hold power in England during the reign of Edward VI (1547 – 1553), which began soon after she joined the Dorsets, and again in the reign of Elizabeth I (1553 – 1603). Bess would maintain these friendships assiduously and they would stand her in good stead for the rest of her life.

There were the Dorsets themselves, and their daughters, the Ladies Jane, Katherine and Mary Grey. There was also the Marchioness' step-mother and close friend, Katherine, Dowager Duchess of Suffolk, another notable evangelical who remained friends with Bess until Katherine's death in 1580. Of lower rank, but in the long-term of greater influence, there was Sir William Cecil, initially a supporter of Edward Seymour, who as Duke of Somerset and Lord Protector to the new king, would be the most powerful man in England. Cecil and Dorset moved into the orbit of Somerset's successor, John Dudley, Duke of Northumberland, with Dorset being promoted to the dukedom of Suffolk.

In the Suffolk circle, there was also Sir William Cavendish – initially an associate of Thomas Cromwell, who, like many others, had been able to snap up valuable bargains after the Dissolution of the Monasteries, and was a wealthy man. Before long, Bess and Cavendish were married, and she was a wealthy wife, and soon the mother of some eight children.

Bess remained close to the Duke of Northumberland's family – indicated by the name of her second daughter, Temperance. The duke had had a daughter of the same unusual name, which hints that either he or his wife was godparent to Temperance Cavendish. Bess became friends with the Northumberland children, of whom Robert, Ambrose, Mary and Katherine Dudley would go on to play an important part in public life.

On the edge of this circle was King Edward's half-sister, the Lady Elizabeth. Whilst for much of Edward's reign, Elizabeth lived quietly in the country, she was on good terms with her brother, willing to conform to the religious changes implemented during it, and a visitor to the court from time to time. There is no record of when she met Bess, but we can infer that they are likely to have met at court occasions – such as the marriage of Robert Dudley to Amy Robsart in 1550.

Another member of the royal family whom Bess may have met during Edward's reign, was Margaret, Countess of Lennox, cousin to both the king and to her old mistress, Frances. Lady Lennox was seldom in the south, her conservative religious position inclined her to keep well away from London, but she was there during the great court occasion when Marie of Guise, Dowager Queen of Scotland visited. It is likely Bess formed one of the throng of ladies and gentlemen rustled up for the occasion.

The future looked rosy for Bess and Cavendish in 1553, but then came news of the death of the king – and the attempt by the Duke of Northumberland and the Duke of Suffolk to put Suffolk's daughter, Jane, married to Northumberland's son, Guilford, on the throne, in place of Edward's half-sister, the Lady Mary. Bess, of course, knew Jane well, and it is likely that she would have been pleased had the attempt succeeded. Her religious outlook was very different from that of Mary.

The coup failed, and Bess and Cavendish fell under suspicion for complicity, but no action was taken against them. Bess sought to ingratiate herself with Queen Mary by requesting her to stand godmother to her new-born son, Charles Cavendish. With her old network of friends now out of power, imprisoned, and in danger of execution, Bess needed new friends quickly. It's not hard to imagine that she built on whatever acquaintanceship she had with Lady Lennox, who was Queen Mary's closest friend.

Lady Jane and her father were executed following a second insurrection by Suffolk – Bess kept a picture of Jane by her bed for the rest of her life. But she still needed new friends. Lady Jane's sister, Katherine, did not suffer for her father's foolishness, and was given a place in Queen Mary's bedchamber. Bess requested Katherine to stand godmother to her next child – it was a good way to maintain closeness to the Grey family, and to keep in with the queen.

But Bess was careful to keep close to her old friends, too – she invited the Lady Elizabeth, now heir to the throne, unless Queen Mary had a child of her own, to be godmother to yet another daughter, and she continued to keep up with Sir William Cecil, who, although he was not a member of the government had managed, despite his Protestant beliefs, to strike up a warm relationship with Cardinal Pole, the new, Catholic, Archbishop of Canterbury.

It became apparent that the queen would not have a child of her own. Whilst the Lady Elizabeth was not in favour with her sister, Bess, widowed again in 1557, gambled that the queen's health was deteriorating to such an extent that Elizabeth would soon inherit. Along with Cecil she kept closely in touch with the princess, and probably visited her at Hatfield, becoming friendly with Elizabeth's attendants, including Frances, Lady Cobham. This strategy paid off. On Elizabeth's accession in November 1558, Bess was appointed as one of her ladies – she was now in more-or-less daily contact with the source of all honour and wealth – important for a widow with seven children to find places for.

Elizabeth's closest companions were Bess' friends of the early 1555os. Cecil became Secretary, and Elizabeth's senior minister for forty-five years. Lord Robert Dudley was the queen's closest friend, his brother, Ambrose, Earl of Warwick, was also favoured by her, and their sister, Mary Dudley, now Lady Sidney, was another of Elizabeth's ladies.

Bess was at the centre of the most powerful network of friends and connections in England and her favour was sought. Lady Katherine Grey, demoted from her place in the Privy Chamber, may have sought help from Bess when she found herself pregnant following a secret marriage. But Bess was far too canny to get involved in a secret that would offend the queen, and apparently gave Katherine short shrift.

Bess had remarried in 1559, to another well-connected man, Sir William St Loe, who had been one of Elizabeth's gentlemen for many years. The marriage was happy, but short-lived. Widowed again in early 1565, Bess had no need to remarry for money or position, but she managed to find a fourth husband who was extraordinarily powerful and well-connected – George Talbot, 6th Earl of Shrewsbury.

The Talbots had come to prominence in the early fifteenth century, when John *'Old Talbot'* was one of the stars of Henry V's French wars. Granted the earldom of Shrewsbury, the Talbots had intermarried with the other great noble families – Staffords,

Nevilles, Mowbrays and Beauchamps – in the fifteenth century, and Howards, Cliffords, Percies and Dacres in the sixteenth century. Bess was presented with five step-children and it was quickly agreed that there would be cross-marriages with her own children. Her network was spreading far and wide.

In 1568, she wrote to no lesser a personage than the Archbishop of Canterbury, seeking a place for the brother of one of her husband's gentlemen. She assured the archbishop of the young man's religious zeal. The letter was written in the usual flowery style of these types of requests *'wherein, although I must confess myself unable to acquit your goodness already showed, yet shall I think myself greatly beholden unto your grace in this behalf.'* For the archbishop to have one of the queen's premier earl's wives owing him a favour might well be of use later.

The first few years of the Shrewsbury marriage were happy, but then disaster struck. The earl was appointed as the guardian of Mary, Queen of Scots, who was being held in England, against her will. Bess was careful initially to be on good terms with Mary – many considered her to be the heir to the throne, and, if Elizabeth had died suddenly, and Mary had inherited, the way the Shrewsburys and treated her as a prisoner would have had a bearing on their subsequent status.

On the other side of the coin, Bess was requested for favours. In around 1570, the Earl of Rutland, whose aunt Gertrude had been Shrewsbury's first wife, wrote to Bess on behalf of a Mistress Higgins, once in Gertrude's employ, asking Bess to help her to find a post. Whilst it may seem surprising that an earl should bestir himself for the benefit of a former employee of a dead aunt, that was how the system worked – the bonds of service enmeshed both employer and employee.

Time marched on, and by the mid-1570s it appeared that history would repeat itself, with the death of a childless queen. Elizabeth was in good health, but Bess looked to the future. Whilst it was unlikely that Mary of Scotland would inherit the English crown, her son, James VI, King of Scots, probably would. His grandmother was none other than Lady Lennox, whom Bess had known for many years and who was a close friend of another of Bess' old friends, Katherine Willoughby, Dowager Duchess of Suffolk.

Before long, Bess and Lady Lennox had presided over what they claimed was a love-match between Bess' daughter, Elizabeth Cavendish, and Lady Lennox' son, Lord Charles Stuart. This was doubly good for Bess and her daughter. If King James inherited, then her daughter would be his aunt-by-marriage, but if there were objections to a foreign-born king, Lord Charles himself, born in England, was Elizabeth's next male heir.

The queen, predictably, was furious. And this is where Bess' long nurturing of her friends and acquaintances paid off. Shrewsbury wrote to Cecil (now Lord Burghley, but still Elizabeth's first minister) that Bess had no treasonable intentions. The Earl of Huntingdon was deputed to investigate the matter. He and his wife, Katherine Dudley, were old friends, convinced Protestants, and were probably sympathetic to Bess. So, whilst

Catholic Lady Lennox was sent to the Tower, Bess escaped punishment.

But nothing is free, and Bess needed to restore herself to the queen's favour. She wrote to her old friend Lady Cobham, still amongst the queen's attendants, for advice on suitable gifts. She was steered away from money and sent a gift of clothes instead. Bess' half-sister, Elizabeth Wingfield, was also one of the queen's ladies – a position probably procured for her by Bess, and wrote to her sister of how well the queen had received the peace-offering. Wingfield and others had been busy persuading the queen of Bess' loyalty *'your honour (Bess) shall know that after my cousin William and my (Wingfield) careful toil...we have reaped such recompense as could not desire better first her majesty never liked anything you gave her so well the colour and strange trimmings of the garments with the rich and great cost bestowed upon it have caused her to give out such good speeches of my Lord (Shrewsbury) and your Ladyship as I never heard of better.'*

Soon after, Bess spent a season at court, on the best possible terms with Elizabeth and Burghley, and much praised by Lord Robert Dudley, now Earl of Leicester.

The young Lennoxes both died within a few years, leaving a daughter, Lady Arbella Stuart, who was permitted to remain with Bess after Lady Lennox' death. Whilst having a potential heir to the throne in her hand seemed initially to be a dream come true for Bess, as time passed, it became a nightmare, as did her once happy marriage to Shrewsbury.

The strain of guarding the Queen of Scots destroyed Shrewsbury's mental well-being, and his marriage. For reasons that are not entirely clear, Shrewsbury took against his wife, and began to accuse her of trying to defraud him. This was not helped by Shrewsbury's finances deteriorating sharply, whilst Bess seemed to make money with everything she touched, refusing to allow him to reduce any of the payments he was due to make to her under their various marriage settlements. She and Queen Mary also fell out and Shrewsbury was at his wits' end.

Soon, the scandal of the Shrewsbury's marital breakdown was so widely known that the queen ordered an investigation. Once again, Bess could rely on her network of friends to help her. Leicester wrote to Shrewsbury, telling him to make peace with his wife. Matters deteriorated, and Shrewsbury made a formal complaint against his wife to the Privy Council. Leicester, still sympathetic to his old friend, paid her a visit to hear her side of the story.

Queen Mary was also bitter against Bess now – perhaps seeing that Bess planned to use Arbella to cut both Mary and James from the succession. With accusations flying about that Shrewsbury and Mary were lovers, Elizabeth convened a hearing. Bess travelled to London where she was warmly received by Elizabeth and all her friends at court. The hearing resulted in Shrewsbury finally being relieved of the burden of the Scots queen, but this did not lead to reconciliation with Bess. Instead, he sought separation.

For Bess, such a step would have been a calamity. In a world where a woman's rank and honour was heavily dependent on that of her husband, to be cast off would be a disgrace. Now, she needed the support of everyone she had ever befriended. The commission to investigate found entirely in Bess' favour, and over the following years, as Shrewsbury refused to take her back to the marital home, repeated investigations found for Bess. Her investment in people paid off.

With the execution of Queen Mary in 1587, Bess began to put more hope in Arbella's future, and cultivated a new generation of courtiers – Burghley's son, Sir Robert Cecil; Leicester's step-son, the Earl of Essex, and another of the queen's favourites, Sir Walter Raleigh. Whilst this did not have the desired effect of encouraging support for Arbella as a potential queen, it did ease Arbella's situation when Elizabeth died, and James of Scotland became of England. Arbella, however, did not learn from her grandmother's example of pragmatism, and careful cultivation of her network, and came to a tragic end.

Chapter 19: Dowries and Marriage Settlements

Bess began her life in dire financial circumstances – the laws relating to underage heirs, to marriage, inheritance and women's property rights influenced everything she did. A clever and practical woman, she used the law to protect herself and her family and to build a huge inheritance for the dynasty she founded.

*

Marriage and Money

Marriage in the Tudor period was primarily a business arrangement. The purpose was to create a functioning economic unit, into which children could be born, and which, hopefully over time, amassed more wealth. For all but the poorest levels of society, agreeing the financial arrangements before the vows were taken was an important step. What is described in this chapter is the general structure in England, of course individual arrangements might be different.

There are four basic points to consider: the dowry (sometimes referred to, especially for royal women as the 'dot(e)'; the jointure; the dower; and the will.

Women and the Law

Under common law, married women had no property rights, everything they owned being the property of their husbands. However, women could be, and usually were, protected by the pre-nuptial marriage articles, which would state the dowry and dower rights, and for well-informed women or careful fathers, exceptions by which she might reserve the right to deal with lands she already held or agree with her husband how her property or lands would be devolved in the event of her pre-deceasing him.

A woman who inherited land, if she managed to emerge from wardship unmarried (a vanishingly small likelihood) could *'sue her livery'* and take possession. Until she married, she would be a *'femme sole'* and have the same rights as a man. Similarly, once widowed, she could operate independently. Queens were *'femmes sole'*, and so, by special Act of Parliament, was Lady Margaret Beaufort, Countess of Richmond and Derby.

Dowry

The dowry was the payment that the bride's family made to the groom's family. It usually consisted of cash and moveable goods, often including livestock. If a man died before his daughters were married, he would usually make provision in his will for dowries for them. This could lead to complications if it was not specified whether each daughter should receive a specific amount, or whether they should share in a single pot of money.

For example, John Hardwick of Hardwick, Bess' father, left a sum of money for dowries for his daughters, mentioning five, who were to have 40 marks apiece. But if his pregnant wife was to bear another daughter, she would also be entitled to 40 marks, and if any of the girls died before marriage, the same sum of money was to be shared amongst the survivors.

Dowries for royal women could be extensive. Mary, daughter of Henry VII, had a dote of 300,000 crowns – around £60,000 – in 1514. Marie of Guise took 100,000 crowns to Scotland in 1536.

Katharine of Aragon's dowry was 200,000 scudos (c. 200,000 crowns). She took part of it in cash, and part in plate and jewels.

Anne of Cleves' marriage treaty specified a dowry of 100,000 gold florins (£16,500 at the time), of which 40,000 was to be paid down, and the remainder after a year.

The dowry became the property of the groom's family. For royal marriages, there might be an agreement that if the husband died, and there were no children, the dowry would revert to the bride or her family. This was the basis in the 1530s for negotiations around a possible dowry for the Lady Mary, the daughter of Henry VIII and Katharine of Aragon. As her parents' marriage was held to be invalid, it was argued that she was entitled to her mother's dowry, which she could take to a potential husband.

Jointure

The jointure was, originally, the land and/or income that was settled on the couple, usually by his father. For an elder son, this would be for the father's life-time, as on the father's death, the eldest son would inherit the whole estate, subject to life-interests (q.v.). For a younger son, the land would remain to him and his wife. It might be entailed on their children or return to the main estate after the son's death. Often, a jointure was held '*in survivorship*', that is, whilst the land was settled on the pair jointly, it would be held by the survivor after being widowed.

Thus, the term *'jointure'* was often used interchangeably with *'dower'* (q.v.).

It was generally held that that part of the jointure held in survivorship should be proportionate to the dowry, and around 10% was commonly thought of as a benchmark. This could differ significantly if the woman brought land as well as money. It would also reflect the social status of the bride. If a lower status man was capturing the daughter of an important man, it was expected that her jointure would be proportionately much higher to reflect the non-tangible benefits of the match.

An example given by Barbara Harris in *'Aristocratic Women 1450-1550: Marriage and Family, Property and Careers'*, is that of the two daughters of Thomas Wriothesley, Earl of Southampton and a Privy Councillor. Anne, marrying a man with no title, had a dowry of 450 marks, and was assigned a jointure of nearly 300 marks per annum. Elizabeth, marrying an Earl's son, took 1,600 marks as dowry but had a much smaller jointure proportionately – 500 marks per annum.

Failure to pay the dowry would result in the wife not receiving her jointure. This was at the root of Katharine of Aragon's problems during her widowhood. It had been agreed that half the dowry would be paid at her marriage with Arthur, and the other half a year later. In return, she was to be secured a jointure of one-third of the revenues of Wales and Cornwall. When Arthur died within a few months of the marriage, the fathers, Henry VII and Ferdinand of Aragon, fell to wrangling.

Ferdinand had not paid all of the dowry, so Henry felt justified in not settling the jointure on Katharine – he was horrified at the thought of such a large revenue being in the hands of his widowed daughter-in-law who might live for fifty years, and would be entitled to it even if she remarried. Katharine had no income of her own for the whole period of her widowhood and was reduced to pawning the jewels and plate that was supposed to form part of the dowry.

Ferdinand eventually paid up in 1509, after Katharine married the new king, Henry VIII.

A woman who married without her father's consent would be unlikely to receive any dowry. This was a strong disincentive to love matches.

In Italy, the custom was for the bride's dowry and goods to be carried to her new home in beautiful painted chests called 'cassone'.

Dower

Under common law in England, if no other provision had been made, a widow was entitled to one-third of the income from the estate as '*dower*'. The purpose was to maintain her, and any younger children for whom there was no separate allocation of land or goods. Frequently, jointure in survivorship was granted on the basis that the widow would forgo her dower rights. Dower was one of the most frequent bones of contention amongst families.

In an age when many people were widowed and remarried, it was not unusual for a son by a first marriage to have a step-mother the same age, or younger, than himself. One third of the income of the estate would be due to her for the rest of her life. There might even be several widows at the same time, each due a proportion. There are numerous court cases where step-mothers, and even natural mothers, complain that the heir is refusing to honour their dower rights.

The case of Bess of Hardwick was fairly typical. She married Robert Barlow when he was a minor. They had no children, and his inheritance rights passed to his younger brother, who, also being a minor became a ward of Sir Peter Frecheville. Frecheville refused to pay Bess her dower, probably claiming that Bess and Robert's marriage had been unconsummated and was therefore voidable (although not void).

Bess took Frecheville to court. He offered a compromise, whereby she would renounce her dower rights for a small settlement. With no money and no powerful friends to back her, Bess was initially forced to accept it, but her late husband's uncle intervened to have the settlement overturned and Bess eventually received her dower, together with some compensation.

The term dower was also used to refer to the lands that kings settled on their wives, similar to the *'jointure'*, except that the lands were assigned to the queen herself, rather than them being held in common with the king. Again, it was the custom that the dower should be proportionate to the dowry, but what the levels were varied between countries.

French queens received a dower of lands worth around 50 – 60,000 livres tournois per annum. Mary the French Queen, was entitled to some £10,000 per annum as the widow of Louis XII. After her marriage to Charles Brandon, Duke of Suffolk, she was obliged to remit £4,000 per annum to her brother, Henry VIII as a suitable punishment for marrying without his consent. Since she had no children with Louis XII, Mary was entitled to the full return of her dote, but Henry took that as well.

Anne of Cleves received a dower under the marriage articles of 1539 of 5,000 marks (£3,300) per annum, which was to be reduced to 3,750 marks if she were to be widowed and return to Cleves. Under the settlement made when the marriage was annulled, she received a similar amount as a pension.

In the 1520s, when Henry VIII was negotiating the proposed dot and dower for his daughter Mary as a wife for the Emperor, a dot of 100,000 crowns was offered, in return for 20,000 crowns per annum. The Imperial negotiators thought this too high – they considered a 10% return to be adequate.

Life interest

A life interest was the legal right to occupy or derive rents from land for the duration of the beneficiary's life. It would cease on his or her death. A father might bequeath an unmarried daughter a life-interest in land by way of charge on her brother's inheritance – this would be most likely to happen where he did not have enough ready cash to make a bequest of capital. The brother could not alienate the land without making suitable alternative arrangements, to which, of course, she might not agree.

As noted above, a widow would have a life-interest in the heir's lands. Bess of Hardwick arranged with her second and third husbands, Sir William Cavendish and Sir William St Loe, that, rather than having a dower of one-third of their estates, she would have a life-interest in the whole. The benefit of this, apart from making Bess personally secure, was that, if her husband died whilst the heir was a minor, there would be no surplus income over her life-interest for any guardian, so it would be unlikely that anyone would seek to be granted the wardship of the under-age heir, allowing Bess to remain in control.

Wills

Until 1536 in England, land could not pass by will – it devolved in accordance with the feudal structure. After that date, half of a holding that was not already entailed, could be passed as the testator saw fit. Wills therefore generally deal with moveable goods and cash until that time.

A married woman could not make a legally binding will without her husband's consent unless the right had been reserved to her in the marriage articles. Of course, she could make an informal will, directing disposal of her property, which her husband might honour. Widows and femmes sole had the same rights as men.

Chapter 19: Book Review

Two biographies of Bess of Hardwick have been written in the last twenty years, one by Mary S. Lovell, and one by David Dunant. Bess also features as a walk-on part in many histories of the Elizabethan age.

Title: Bess of Hardwick: First Lady of Chatsworth

Author: Mary S. Lovell

Publisher: Abacus

In a nutshell   A meticulous and detailed account of Bess of Hardwick's life from cradle to grave.

Mary S. Lovell is an accomplished biographer, whose oeuvre stretches from the Mitford sisters to Amelia Earhart. Her biography of Bess of Hardwick takes her back further in time than any of her other works, but she has delved into a wealth of sources to give us a thorough picture of Bess. Like so many women who dare to stand up for the rights, or to have ambitions on their own account, Bess has often been vilified as a shrew and a Tudor gold-digger, but Lovell paints a much more nuanced picture.

To promote your family, to marry well, and to increase your wealth were fundamental mores of Tudor society. Bess managed to do all these things without being born into a family of wealth or influence. Lovell shows us how Bess learnt from the financial straits her father's early death left her mother in to use the law to fight for her own rights.

The information about Bess' four marriages is also full of interest - in particular, the use of letters and contemporary documents to show that, far from being a harpy, Bess was genuinely attached to her husbands, and they to her.

The ins-and-outs of the legal quarrels surrounding the estates of Bess' third husband, Sir William St Loe, are both new in terms of biographies of Bess, and also interesting – Lovell, by pure coincidence, is married to a man connected to the St Loe family, and found new documentary sources in their own family archives.

Lovell explores the breakdown of Bess' fourth marriage to the Earl of Shrewsbury. She shows the unbearable strain put on their relationship by the guardianship of Mary, Queen of Scots. Interestingly, she also explodes the myth that Bess quarrelled with Elizabeth I, pointing out that despite diligent efforts, she has found no contemporary evidence of such a quarrel.

The character of Bess comes across extremely well – Lovell is obviously an admirer, but it is not hard to see in Bess how financial insecurity drove her all her life, and how she later used her money to control her family – although they loved her, she dominated them by holding the purse-strings.

The saddest part of the story is the breakdown in the relationship between Bess and her granddaughter, Arbella. Bess had played for high stakes in arranging a secret marriage between her daughter and a potential heir to the throne, and she paid the price when she had to witness Arbella's increasing frustration and despair.

The book is not a light read, you need to concentrate, and keep focus, but it is very rewarding.

Bibliography

Durant, David N, *Bess of Hardwick: Portrait of an Elizabethan Dynast* (London: Littlehampton Book Services, 1977)

de Lisle, Leanda, *The sisters who would be queen the tragedy of Mary, Katherine, & Lady Jane Grey* (Glasgow: HarperCollins e-books, 2008)

Lovell, Mary S, *Bess of Hardwick: First lady of Chatsworth* (London: Little, Brown & Company, 2005)

Marshall, Rosalind Kay K, *Queen Mary's Women: Female Relatives, Servants, Friends and Enemies of Mary, Queen of Scots* (Edinburgh: John Donald Publishers, 2006)

Public Record Office, *Calendar of State Papers: Domestic Series: Edward VI, 1547-1553* (United Kingdom: Stationery Office Books, 1992)

https://www.bessofhardwick.org *The complete correspondence, 1550-1608* (2013),

Whitelock, Anna, *Elizabeth's Bedfellows*, Kindle edn (London: Bloomsbury Publishing PLC, 2013)

http://www.british-history.ac.uk/cal-cecil-papers

Printed in Dunstable, United Kingdom